# MY CHRISTIAN JOURNEY THROUGH A FALLEN WORLD

SARAH TYLER

Publishing Coordinator – Sharon Kizziah-Holmes

Paperback-Press
an imprint of A & S Publishing
A & S Holmes, Inc.

ISBN -13: 978-1-945669-74-3

# DEDICATION

To The King and His Kingdom

## ACKNOWLEDGMENTS

Special thanks to Sharon at Paperback Press
for her patience and spiritual insight into my
heart of writing.

# CONTENTS

# FORWARD

*My heavenly Father, thank You for how You have brought me through all these years, I love You so very much and I want to tell the world in this new book.*

The Christian life is not what so many think when they hear someone telling how they are going to heaven when they die. I now know how important that is but, it took many years and lots of valleys before I got to that point and beyond to my Christian journey.

I want to share this story of that life and all I found to be true as I begin this journey. What I was told from the beginning, my birth, until I could remember for myself, the struggles of life. Why is my story worthy to write and for you to read? Because I believe you will find yourself in at least one of the chapters, and possibly in several. And you hopefully will grow in your walk with the Lord and perhaps not make some of the mistakes I made. That you will also see that God does have a purpose and plan for every life. *For once you were blind, but now you see* (John. 9:25).

## THIS IS MY CHRISTIAN JOURNEY THROUGH A FALLEN WORLD.

*How long wilt thou forget me O Lord? Forever? How long wilt thou hide thy face from me? How long shall I take counsel in my soul, having sorrow in my heart daily? How long shall my enemy be exalted over me? Consider and hear me, O Lord my God: lighten mine eyes lest I sleep the sleep of death. Lest my enemy say. I have prevailed against him: and those that trouble me rejoice when I am moved. But I have trusted in thy mercy: my heart shall rejoice in thy salvation. I will sing unto the Lord, because He hath dealt bountifully with me* (Psalms13: 1-6).

When you know the heart of God and you know how much He loves you, then you can get a handle on this fact; whatever He has for you is the best, and you know to trust that purpose and plan, no matter how you feel or how much it may hurt. I experienced this on my journey.

# INTRODUCTION

Can you imagine a little child in the midst of 6 older children, and then later three younger ones, and with ten children being in a household of poor, needy and dysfunctional family?

That's what I grew up in. I know Mommy and Daddy really meant well, but with so many mouths to feed and so many bills to pay, we just didn't get the attention that all children require to grow up and become ALL God plans them to be. That is until God takes total control of our lives, and that happens when we realize that *we are not our own, we are bought with a price*

(1. Corinthians 6:20).

I was one of ten Thomas kids that needed and actually craved attention. From the very beginning I needed to be recognized, and always sought to stand out in a crowd. I just didn't get that attention.

Maybe that's why I involved myself in many different avenues. I stood out at school; I was a good student and was known for my achievements. For example; I loved to make my reports that handed in to be well presented. Nice folder with special emblems on the cover, etc.

I needed to feel important. I am amazed that I didn't get into the "wrong crowd" always wanting to be important and accepted, but that had to be only because "God had His plan for me".

I want to ask you right now, "Do you understand that God has a plan for you"? It will make so much more sense as you start to understand this.

The Christian Journey, contrary to some, saying, "It is for the weak and even calling those that need a crutch to get through life." It is actually for the strong, persistent, and mighty individuals. The difference being that *the believer in Jesus as Savior, knows from whom comes their strength* (Psalms 28:7).

As I take you on this journey through these pages I hope to help you see how all that I express on this journey has and is, all through the power of Jesus.

When I was born I, like you never knew what lay ahead for me on my life journey. I, like you was not a mistake, but a planned purpose of our great Creator. He knew our lives from the foundation of the world. Sounds unbelievable? Well I am about to explain to you how this is truth.

Get out your Holy Bible. I will be using scripture from the King James Version. If you have other translations feel free to follow God's word. The word is breathed into the scriptures through the writing of the author by the Holy Spirit.

# CHAPTER ONE

## *The Beginning Journey: Christ has His Plan*

*For I know the thoughts that I think toward you, saith the Lord, thoughts of peace, and not of evil, to give you an expected end. The Lord in His Holy Word says I have a Purpose and a Plan for you (*Jeremiah 29:11).

July 2, 1943 was a hot, sunny day when this story started to unfold. You know, that kind of day when someone might say, "Well the 4th of July is near what kind of plans should we make for this great Independence Day celebration?" My family could tell you what happened on July 2, 1943, but I can too. I have heard this story many times from family members as they recalled the life that began on that day. My life, Sarah Thomas Tyler--the author of this true story.

I'd like to tell you what I was told about my birth, and things *I've* learned through life. You may ask, "Why do I want to read about someone I don't even know?" To find yourself.

You see, I've had events that will take you through the whys and whats of this thing we call life. We that are born will go on this journey. It's not by accident that you are reading this; it is meant to help you find comfort and discover, "Just why and what it is all about." I hope it shows you there is a purpose and a plan.

So we begin on July 2, 1943.

A loud screech of anxiety and pain shrieked through the air. A strong cry was heard by my siblings, "Go get your dad from the shop! Right now! This one does not want to wait for the doctor." While in intense pain, Momma cried for anyone to help.

She lay there in the tiny bedroom of the very small, indiscreet home on Kearney Street. The home part was behind a small building with a grocery store on one end and a restaurant on the other, which was the livelihood of the Thomas family.

By then there were three sisters and three brothers. I was trying to enter this old world as number seven. What in the world was Momma and Daddy thinking, having this many kids? Didn't they know what caused children? Did they really want this many children? We all know back then there was really no good plan to keep from getting pregnant. So, there were three more to follow me. Gosh!!! Must be why all of us kids that married only had one or two at the most. (Except my sister Susan, she had four).

Susan and Bonnie, the two older girls, hastened

to momma's cry and command. Bonnie ran to get Daddy from the radio/machine shop that set at the back part of the property, another means of our income, while Susan called the doctor.

Doctors came to the house back then for deliveries, and eight of the ten children were birthed at home.

Momma cried out again, "Tell the doctor he better hurry, this one is fighting to come out."

I didn't know all that lay ahead of me from that hot summer day in July. If I had, I doubt I would have wanted to come out!

Never the less ready or not, here I came. I did not wait for the doctor to arrive they say, but he did manage to get there in time to cut the cord. Oh, that life line.

The doctor checked me over. "It's another girl," he said. Then Momma says, "What are we going to name her?"

I was told in my later years everyone there offered suggestions.

"We have Susan, Bonnie, and Peggy, let's name her Sarah." Momma picked the name.

My oldest brother Junior said, "I want her name to be Louise. That's my girlfriend's name."

"Oh, you may not even have her as girlfriend next week," momma was quoted as saying. "But we can use that for her middle name."

There you go; Sarah Lou (Louise) Thomas. Me. I was officially in this world and as everyone does, I started my earthly journey.

That journey through a fallen world. The other three were born over the next four years. Katy,

Richard and baby girl, Dixie. About time to quit since momma was now 46 years old.

Momma, Daddy and ten children. We made up the Thomas Clan.

I grew into a dark-haired, some say tender hearted, lanky, small in stature girl. I was a good student in school and loved to play house with my sisters. Little did I know that my life and purpose of God was in its beginning?

*My heavenly Father, I didn't even know you at this point in my life. But I want to praise you and give you all glory for what happened later on. Thank You for the plan that you had for me to include me in your great calling.*

Though academically I was good in school, it was difficult for me in other ways. It was especially difficult during my elementary years because I had asthma and we could not afford to go see doctors. I suffered with breathing problems, and often I would have to prop myself up in bed at night to get any sleep. I was plagued by one cold after another, which also added to my respiratory distress, but I tried to pretend I was okay so I would be like other kids my age. Nobody wants to be different.

I had chosen to volunteer to sell milk at school. I sat at the table where kids came through for lunch hour to get their milk. Every day I used this opportunity to pass the half bag of Fritos to my sister when she came through the line. I had already had my lunch, and because we were so poor, this way maybe no one would know we didn't have our own bag of chips. It's sad for a child to have to disguise the 'lack of money' in an effort to appear normal. Who defined 'normal' anyway?

My daddy said selling and handling the cold milk in the draft of the doorway was why I always had a cold. Could that be true? I didn't know and just accepted that Daddy was right. But I didn't give up selling milk. I was used to being sick.

I bet our family would have qualified for so much assistance back then, but Daddy was a proud man and wouldn't accept help. The secret he held may have been part of his reasoning. You will hear about the secret and how sad, if only he had known.

I was as shy and introverted as a young child. I pretty much kept to myself. My older sisters watched over me and protected me if someone tried to push me around. God's plan again. We all walked together to school about one and half miles. (So to all the young kids out there, when grandma says this, it was true for some of us.)

My older sister Bonnie always wanted to stop by this one friend's house to pick her up then continue our final walk... Bonnie's friend had a sister that was special needs. She would walk around and shake a paper bag by me. I didn't know she would not hurt me. For a child who didn't understand such things it was pretty scary to me at the time.

I had several fears. I was afraid of cows. I would not walk past one and I definitely wouldn't go into a pasture where they were. Ick!

My oldest sister, Susan had a plan to cure me of this. One day she said we were going to walk through the pasture behind our house to cut through on our way to the store.

I said, "I can't take that!"

"I'll carry you on my back," Susan said. "Just close your eyes until we get past the cows."

"Okay." I hopped on her back and closed my eyes. I had to trust her, didn't I?

After a while she said, "Okay we are back into the woods past the pasture open your eyes.

I opened my eyes and she had me right beside a big, black and white Jersey cow. I screamed and the cow jumped back. The cow did not really appear to be hurtful; in fact the animal seemed to be afraid of me. You know what? I wasn't afraid anymore. My sister had helped me confront and conquer that fear.

The unknown becomes the fears in our lives, once we have confirmation and know we will be safe after all, most times those fears will dissipate. Wish I had known the following verse back when I was young and afraid.

*I will never leave You or forsake You* (Hebrews 13:5).

*Lord You know my heart. You know that I need thee every hour. As I begin this next chapter on my difficult life, I acknowledge that if it had not been for You, Jesus, it could have ended differently. Even though I didn't know You at this stage of my life, you knew me and were guiding me to You on my path. Thank You Jesus!*

### *Moving on with this Journey*

I would like to fast forward to 1956. I was

thirteen years old and attended Study Junior High in Springfield, MO. Oh, those teenage years. I looked like I was about ten because I was so small. I was always told 'you're all legs'.

My daddy had carnival stuff at that time. You'll read more about it in the chapter Carnival Life, 'Wouldn't You Like to Know?' I loved to do trapeze/gymnastics. I remember well flying through the air from a high bar, part of a structure of my daddy's ride equipment.

I know God's purpose and plan was unfolding for my life, but it didn't seem like it at the time. However, I felt God's love when I sat and talked with my maternal Grandma Madden. I later learned she was a "believer in Jesus Christ".

Each year at Christmas, Grandma brought a bible to give to the next child in line of the family. When my time came I was given a smaller bible. I wondered why my brothers and sisters got big bibles. Then I realized that was silly because God's word is God's word.

So did I read it? No, I tried but didn't understand it. Did that change God's great purpose and plan for my life? No. He was still in control and leading me ever so gently on the great journey.

One day some folks from a nearby church came by our home and told Momma, "If you will let the children come to Sunday school, we'll pick them up and they can get a bible."

I wanted to go so badly. If only to get a bigger bible than what Grandma Madden gave me. Momma would not let us go and I wondered why? Maybe it was *the* secret.

*Lord, You know our thoughts; You know our words even before we speak them. I am so grateful for Your boundless love and mercy to me.*

As I am writing this book, I am reflecting on my Grandma Madden and how I loved to visit with her. She was instrumental in my loving to write. I used to write to her from our summer travels when we were on the Carnival circuit. You will read about this in Chapter Three. I told her in letters so many exciting things that would happen. Those letters were long and I had so much enthusiasm. I wrote the scary times and the far-fetched dangers we encountered as we went from town to town.

I might write something like, *Grandma, we almost had a snake from the snake side show get-out, and it was found pretty close to going into the trailer house of my sisters and me!*

Grandma would write back and say, *really? Did you ALMOST capture it?*

She knew I liked to make it interesting so she went along with my *big* story.

Funny, how your life is your destiny just by how you start out in areas you never knew would lead to that destiny.

My love to write to my grandma, as I said, was one of the things that led me to writing. It was the beginning of this area of my life. I thank her for that.

Today I find it easy to write on social media. I like to reply to my friends posts. I guess maybe I have replied too much at times. Sometimes I say things that are taken out of context.

But then, there you go. Isn't that what happens in all our conversation today? No one writes, or maybe I should say, no one reads what you write in the same light you meant it. Unfortunately, you can't hear voice inflection in writing, so sometimes you might simply write the word 'sure' and someone would take it like a bland, 'well, okay… I guess' instead of 'I think that would be great!' like you intended it to be.

Let's use today's political realm as an example. We do not hear, see, read or interpret what is said, in the same context as others. We all have our opinion of the meaning of what happens. So, don't worry about how *you* are interpreted. We are who we are and that's pretty hard to change, even if we may want to change.

I personally want everyone to know I say what I mean and mean what I say, so there you go.

## Chapter Two

***In the Mist of Life: A Lost Child Needs Attention***

As I mentioned, the Thomas clan was so very, very poor. At least at this time of my life I knew no difference, but somehow didn't grasp the seriousness of it. I remember large bushels of apples, potatoes, big pots of soup, which were actually more water than ingredients, but never the less we always had food to eat. How hard it must have been for Momma and Daddy to provide for all of us children.

When I started junior high school I began to see something in our lives was different. I didn't have all the "stuff" my friends had. I wasn't allowed to have any friends come to my house. I was told, I had enough brothers and sisters to be with, and I didn't need friends. It was hard for me to understand, but that's when I started to really realize how poor we were. I accepted that but kept on having friends at *school* only. I made countless excuses about why they couldn't ever come over to our house. It was hard on a teenager.

Do you remember being sixteen? Did you have dreams of being important? Maybe even a movie star?

At sixteen, I saw that I had a musical talent to offer. I loved to sing. I really thought I would be a Rock 'N Roll star someday. NOT! This was not part of God's purpose and plan. However, that didn't stop me from loving to perform and I'd do that anywhere anyone would let me. I sang mainly country but my dream was to sing Connie Francis style. (For those that do remember her, she was hot in the '50s'. Look her up on YouTube.)

At school I always asked if I could be in the school program. I wanted to sing every chance I got. My teachers would always allow me to sing at the earliest opportunity. The Thomas clan had so many kids, how could our parents pay attention to each one of us? I think school personnel recognized I needed to feel important in some way because at home I didn't feel loved or appreciated.

I guess I was searching, even back then, to get into the 'purpose and plan' God had for me, so I started entering beauty pageants. I don't know how many times I heard, 'life is hard', 'money don't grow on trees', 'get out there and help your brothers with the painting'… The one that got me most was, "Who do you think you are? You think you're beautiful? Well, you can't eat a beauty trophy, little lady!"

That's true, but those pageants helped boost my self-esteem. Fun to be in the Pageants.

*Competitions for Miss Missouri*

Swimsuit

Evening Gown

Talent

Talent

Why did I enter? It wasn't because I thought I was beautiful, I wanted to promote my singing. That rock and roll star in me just didn't want to give up! I was one of 10 finalists in Miss Springfield, and later a finalist in Miss Missouri. I so enjoyed being a part of these pageants. But God had other plans.

I did, however, get to sing on the Ozark Jubilee TV show. It was so exciting! All the cameras, the backup singers and dancers...but to get to meet the host Red Foley in person...wow!

That could have been a start of my budding singing career, but again Daddy stepped in and would not allow it. Was it because of that deep dark secret they were hiding? I didn't know and didn't care.

My heart was broken and I think Momma knew it. Now, Momma was more thoughtful.

She told me one time, "You're such a pretty young girl and someday a boy will sweep you away and change your life."

What, Momma complimented me? It stuck in my mind forever. Momma thought I was pretty.

I wish I had asked if being swept off my feet was a good thing or bad. I wondered if maybe she was sad because of how her life had turned out; how it was so changed by Daddy. Maybe she felt she missed out on a good life? Had he swept her off her feet, then kept her 'barefoot and pregnant', as the saying goes?

All I know is, from my experiences, God has a purpose and plan for everyone. Since things went in the direction they did for Momma, I accept this was God's plan for her.

*God knows our name, and God You knew me as You knit me together in my momma's womb. Psalms 139; 13 KJV. I am not a mistake Lord and I am surrounded by Your love.*

*My heavenly father, I know You knew all about our lives back then also, and I thank You that You kept me and protected me from harm's way. What a great God You are!!*

## *Lesson*

You wouldn't think from this beginning and all the poor and hopeless struggles I've had, that God was watching after me or still had His plan and purpose for my life. Never give up because He does, for each of us that enter this old, and now, fallen world. I call it a fallen world because *in the beginning God created the heavens and the earth* (Genesis 1:1).

He also tells us it was good. He created Adam from the dust of the ground and saw that Adam needed a help mate. Enter Eve. They lived in a beautiful paradise.

God then created the birds of the air, the land and sea animals. God always said it was good. He also created the angels. From what the scriptures tell us there was the good, the bad and the ugly angels. Satan was the highest angel God created.

Before he became Satan he was the arch angel. But just like us, as God's creations, Michael the arch angel, had his own agenda. To be like God? That could never be. God is The Almighty God there is no other. I will be showing you how over the years the world went from good to bad, and as we keep traveling along it becomes very bad.

### *How Far are We Falling?*

In the 1950's for example, the TV shows we viewed said a lot. Those shows taught children how to behave, moral values and what family life was like.

We watched shows like I Love Lucy; Andy Griffith, Father Knows Best, Leave it to Beaver and children's shows like Howdy Doody, Rin Tin Tin and movies with Shirley Temple. These shows were not only entertaining, but they taught us how to be courteous, respectful, responsible and more. We'd sing songs like; Old King Cole, Hickory Dickory Dock and Hey Diddle Diddle. When we got a little older it was songs like; I Found My Thrill on Blueberry Hill, Young Love, You Light Up My life, Rocking Around the Christmas Tree, My Boyfriend's Back and You're Going to be in Trouble and It's My Party and I'll Cry if I Want to…look them up on YouTube, You might enjoy the music of the '50's.

All very innocent and fun songs. I knew most of these songs because I sang in school parties with some bands. But time goes on and all changes.

TV shows have become radical, even back in the day, you'd have to watch daytime soaps in privacy, (I know now shouldn't even watch in privacy. Did you ever think you would see two men rolling around in bed on daytime TV? Or, a man and woman having sex in bed on TV?) God, what is happening?

And the music over the last few years is so unsavory. Cuss words and bad thoughts are sent out to the listeners. Sex runs rampant in the lyrics, killing and no respect for life vibrates through the speakers. The world declines into the fallen world I am writing about.

Now if you see things different than I do I understand, because you are viewing the happenings through your own eyes? Try looking from the perspective of The Great Creator. Remember, The Great One has that purpose and plan for *your* life. So follow along with me and I'll try to help you understand why, from the beginning, we have been headed for this fallen world.

### *The Great Fall*

Picture this scene; most of us are aware of Adam and Eve, the paradise garden that God created for them to enjoy and have all God prepared for them. EXCEPT: One rule. *Eat of anything you desire in the garden, but do not eat of the one tree that I have instructed you to not touch, the tree of good and evil* (Genesis 2.16-17). Adam is *The Man*, God created him to be strong and responsible. Eve was only to be Adam's help mate, the weaker vessel.

What has happened to *The Man* in the families? Life was meant for the man that God created first to be the head of the house. But, when the man would not take his responsibilities, then the woman, mother had to take over. We were to be the man's help mate, not the provider and head of the family.

Picture this scene; Eve wanders off into the

garden and standing by a tree, in comes a slithering serpent indwelled by Satan I'm sure. It introduces itself to Eve in a cunning way:

*"Have you eaten of every tree in this beautiful garden?"*

*Eve answers, "Yes all but the one tree that God has instructed us to never eat of it, or we will surly die"* (Genesis 3:11).

The serpent then says, *"Oh you will not surely die, God just doesn't want you to eat of the tree of knowledge because then you will have your eyes opened and you will see that you can be all you are meant to be."*

Ha!! This is where the big lie comes in and changes the whole course of our history. Read about this temptation in Genesis 3:1-7. Eve succumbs to the temptation and that's where the beautiful plan and purpose of God starts its downfall. This is where you and I also have our trouble, when we do not obey our creator and start on our own journey without God.

Don't beat yourself up at this point however, because you and I didn't have anything to do with what Eve did that started the fallen world. (Actually, it was the main fault of Adam.) This is from a woman's point of view, you understand.

And the reason it was Adam's fault? God created the heaven and the earth, made the beautiful home for Adam to live in. When he created the animals He gave Adam the purpose to name each animal. Adam was God's *Man*. He had the luxury of being God's creation and the *responsibility* of all decisions. So when God created Eve for Adam,

Adam was the responsible person because he was God's Man.

Even though she offered the forbidden fruit to Adam to eat like she did, why didn't he stand up as *God's man*? He should have said, *"NO, God said not to eat of this one fruit of the forbidden tree. As for me and my house we will serve the Lord"* (Joshua 24:14-15). You and I are part of it because of Adam and Eve's sin.

Hypothetically, if we knew what dogs think, you might have a dog outside on a five acre fenced lot. He could run and run yet be protected from the dangers that are outside the fence. However, the dog might reach the outer fence and wonder what was outside those five acres. He has all he needs, food, water, love of family, a fence to keep the wild animals out and much more. It's his own little paradise, but he still wanders outside the fence to explore. Why?

We are the same way, never satisfied or content with the paradise we have. We want more. Greed?

So now you are aware of what started the downfall of God's beautiful creation. When disobedience happened and sin entered--the fall began.

Over the years, I felt my life progressively became worse. I thought it was just the way life happened.

# CHAPTER THREE

***My Carnival Life:***
***There's more to this Business than You Think***

We had just torn down all the rides and concessions in Marshfield and had another journey to make. The sound of stillness surrounded me as we traveled down the long and desolate highway heading for another town. We would set up all the carnival rides, shows and concessions again in many little towns.

This was a crazy life, this carnival life. Daddy, Momma, two brothers and three sisters, at this time, were part of this traveling band of "carnies" as we were called.

I felt like a celebrity when we arrived in the different towns and set everything up. It was so exciting to roll into each location. I could hardly wait to see where we would be located in each place. It could be a city park, or the Fairgrounds. Sometimes we would end up in my least favorite location--the town square.

We'd pulled our trailers into town and parked them right on the street. They'd have to be leveled and connected to some sort of sewer.

I hated when the town's people would stare at us. I knew they were thinking, oh, those poor vagabonds, no home except their trailers, how terrible to have to live like that. But when we got all set up, and my sisters and I were operating our concession; popcorn, snow cones, and cotton candy, well I felt totally different. The young people would come by to purchase and think we were stars. It made me feel better because I craved attention that gave me a sense of importance.

Many people confuse a carnival with a circus. We were a carnival with rides, tents, sideshows, and many other things. A circus of course has animals, elephants, tigers, trapeze stars.

Being an innocent young teenager, I never compared the carnival business with forms of gambling, like Las Vegas types of income. Well, I learned that this is so in carnival life too.

Surprise, surprise!! There is plenty of gambling in the carnival circuit. And there were plenty of politics involved in carnival life during the 1950's.

My dad was, let's say, the politician. He made friends with the fair committee guys of the towns we played. We would come in and set up rides, tents, side shows, etc. Dad, because of part of the deep secret I spoke about, and will speak more in depth about later, had cash money because he didn't turn in monies made from the carnival business. This money was unclaimed income, making it possible for him to smoke big cigars and have cash to bribe the people of influence that would grant his wishes on his agenda.

Dad would take a big cigar, wrap a $100 bill around it then put it into the shirt pocket of the head of the committee. They loved that and let him run any illegal games he wanted. So off he goes to meet the heads of fair committees... Knowing he would get what he wanted. Gambling tents on carnivals are games that were rigged to make sure the carnival owner was the winner they were called gambling concessions. Sometimes, if a large crowd watched a customer play a game, the "flat joint operator" (suave and crooked carnival operator) would let the player win something better or even money so it would entice the others to play. You might as well have been in Las Vegas.

### *What a perverse world we live in. A Fallen World.*

It was sad when I watched all those people play the gambling concessions and lose their money. They would go and get loans from friends, even banks in an effort to win back their money. That was not going to happen. The concessions they played and lost at were like I said folks, RIGGED. That's right they were set to make the carnival owner the WINNER!! Sometimes players would become so angry, they would start a big midway fight.

We as carnies knew to call out, *"hey-rude."*

This would notify all carnies to be on the alert for what might happen. The sheriff would be called and measures would be taken to protect ourselves.

The carnies also had their own private language that enabled them to talk, if they needed to say something in front of the customer, (we called them suckers). That sounds terrible to me now, but that was the carnie way.

Now don't misunderstand, there were some legal games too. They were mild, but still you only won bears, or trinkets. Just like the duck pond. There were numbers on the bottoms of the ducks floating around, but the prizes that were the greatest were not in the lineup of floating ducks.

On the dart balloon game, the balloons were blown so tightly that very few could actually bust three in a row. Yup! That's the way of the carnival life. Sort of like Las Vegas huh?

I know how this works too well. One day while running the balloon game, an expert dart thrower showed up and started to play. The more he played, the more I lost. Each time he played, I would lose another big bear prize. I was horrified at the loss I was taking. There went my profit at the end of the day. He and his friend kept laughing at the discouragement on my face. They knew what they cost me, but they just laughed. They knew exactly how I felt.

I finally had to say, "Oh there is a limit to how many prizes one individual can win at a given time." My disclaimer was a bit late, but effective. Not to say that carnivals of today in 2018 are as dishonest as in our days, but I would lay odds that they are worse--just saying.

***The carnival life was fun at times; we saw lots of
different little towns.***

As a teenager I was able to make more money
than most adults. I always came in from the circuit
each fall with plenty of money. Did I get to control
it? NO! Momma had an envelope with each kid's
name that worked on the carnival. She would put it
away into the home safe. There it stayed, UNLESS
we really could convince momma that we really,
really needed something that we were asking OUR
money for. Then she would give us the twenty
questions routine to see if we really, really needed
what we were asking for.

I guess that's why I am so conservative today.
Far more conservative than my husband. I am a
saver, he is a spender. But that's the way life can be
based on your upbringing. And I learned that money
doesn't grow on trees, I learned that it can be here
today, but gone tomorrow.

Just like when we had a truck break down on one
of the trips from one town to the next.

My brothers needed to get some repairs done,
and well, they needed some cash.

My sisters and I were there along the road
waiting for them and the repair. They asked, "Who
has some money in the trailer?"

Well of course it was the trailer my sisters and I
stayed in, and I kept my saved money in one of the
under bed drawers. I knew they needed help. So,
there went my SAVED money.

You would think that when we got home
Momma and Daddy would replace that spent money

of mine, but that didn't happen. Of course my sisters had no money so that's why mine was used. Did I learn? NO! I still kept saving my hard earned money.

The way Daddy's reasoning on the carnival circuit was--money talks.

Not much different nowadays with the politician's, huh? The big insurance and medical companies, etc. will hire a person (good talker) to go to the different Congressmen, State Representatives and bribe the politician to get what the insurance and big companies want to pass from their votes to set well with big companies' agendas. They are called lobbyists and they work for big companies with that in mind, to get what the large company wants done for them.

They do this using several methods. They may use hush money, or even provide a "lady of the evening" to the politician to have them vote in the big company's favor.

I personally knew of this from a former employer. He had several Nursing Homes, and if he needed to keep regulations, etc. down, he would send the lobbyist he hired to the State Capitol to hob knob with the politicians and then give them what they wanted to promote his agenda. Sad what money or favors will do to get you what you want.

That's why I see the carnival life so much like the political life so similar today. Maybe wasn't always that way, (oh, I think it always was) thank God some cannot be bought.

But Carnival life had its good and bad times.

I am glad that I was out of carnival life as my life changed in the years to come.

## CHAPTER FOUR

*A Big family in turmoil.*

My Situation, not a Normal Family…was yours?

We were able to get this beautiful home in 1952. I lived here from 1952-1965. Then I was able to escape the (commune) dysfunctional home life. For it was a beautiful house, just not a home. A big family can bring lots of different situations. You have your brothers and sisters to run to when the outside world starts to close in but then, you also have the conflict within the family. The Thomas family had the bearing of a family that would be considered a "Dysfunctional, Family" in more ways than one.

Being raised by a tyrant dad and a mother that was afraid of her husband is the beginning of discord and an unnatural family life. You may say that we were like living in a commune, a cult type of setting.

We had no privileges like other kids and we grew to believe this was normal. But as I grew older and witnessed all the dysfunctional family things happening, I  eventually understood that each of us MUST find a way to escape this commune.

Family dinners were very weird. Daddy was king. When we set the table, momma always said, "Be sure dad has his fork, knife, spoon, and an extra sharp knife to cut his meat." A glass of water and butter he wanted had better be in front of him. I watched my mother place margarine into an empty real butter container just so dad would eat it. He had to have REAL butter. But to save money mom played the switch game.

Now, that's not normal. We filed around the table like little Indians, and I remember hoping dad never got mad at something or it would be a terrible time at the table.

Girls in the family were really not held in importance in the same way as the brothers. I guess because the boys were of more value to dad in the work field. The work field consisted of "Dad's world". They never held an outside job, they only worked with dad in some area of the family's

Thomas old home place built 1900

business.

I know it must have been hard to raise and feed all these kids. Dad went from mechanics and radio repair into the carnival world. The boys worked right there with him. Once we were in the carnival world the girls also helped, doing jobs like painting, selling tickets, etc. As bad as I thought it was, the worst was yet to come.

I will tell you about all the 10 children, how and what has happened in each life. Each and every one of us has had our share of tragedy, and now that I look back, I see that it came from being raised in this dysfunctional family environment.

Such a beautiful home, five bedrooms, and mommy and daddy had built on a bathroom off of what used to be a library. We all worked on it for weeks to get it ready. We had two sisters to a bedroom, but the three boys each had their own, and my youngest sister, two year-old Dixie, stayed in mom and dad's room.

Very different from our house on Kearney Street that had beds with boys at one end and girls at the other end—much like an Army barrack. There were two and three kids to a bed also. Whew!

We all felt like millionaires living in this home, especially when we came from living in the house I was born in, with a grocery store/restaurant in front and the little 4 room home in back. Amazing how I really didn't realize how poor we were, even though I wondered how we had money for this big home. Well Dad sold the Kearney St. property and there was the money for this beautiful big home. It didn't change our dysfunctional, commune lifestyle that I assumed was normal. I was never inside other houses to see how they lived since I was not allowed to have friends. The deep dark secret is about to be revealed.

### *Sad Days Ahead: Prison Time*

A knock on the door one morning set the whole Thomas clan upside down. Dad never ever filed income taxes. Part of the big secret. Funny thing is, I didn't know that's why we were always on guard and so secret about our lives. It was tax evasion and kids living under a tyrant Dad.

How he was finally caught I really don't remember, but I do remember the IRS men were at our door before I got home from school. Our whole world came to a screeching stop. The worst thing to come out of this was that my two older brothers had not signed up for the draft which was mandatory back then. That really opened up a can of worms.

I had just gotten home from school and when I walked in and saw two men all dressed in suits, setting at the dining table with momma and daddy. Momma, said." "Go on into the kitchen."

Quickly I went into the kitchen as momma instructed which was extremely unusual. My heart beat so fast I thought I might pass out. Then I saw my sister Bonnie who shuddered against the kitchen wall back in the area where we little Indians all filed in to eat.

When I looked at my sister she actually looked scared. "What's wrong"?

"They have caught Dad after all these years."

At that moment I had no idea why. "What did he do?"

Bonnie looked up. "He's going to prison!"

It was hard to comprehend and I looked back at Bonnie, who looked about as lost as I felt. "Why what has he done?"

Bonnie looked straight at me. "He has never filed income taxes and the IRS is here to take him to prison."

I began to cry with Bonnie while I walked to her and held her close. We both wept profusely about this terrible mess the Thomas clan has found themselves in. I cried for more Thomas problems than I could count, and I will continue to cry over the days ahead. Dad contacted a sharp CPA man to help put all the books in order. Luckily Dad had enough cash stashed away to pay a CPA. When you do not pay your taxes and just kept your money in a home safe you have available cash. But my poor sister Bonnie was the one who had to get all the receipts, documents, and anything that proved income, expenses and supplies together in order to help the CPA.

There were ledgers and spread sheets to put together, any receipts to be located, monies in bank, monies on hand. Needless to say this would be a dark, dark day in the Thomas family.

I didn't know much about paying taxes, or government involvement, but I knew from everything I heard there were big changes coming. I was very afraid.

Oh, what tangled web we weave; when we practice to deceive. Saying it like it was.

The IRS man's voice echoed in my ears while I remained hidden.

"You have 30 days to get your papers in order. And we will be looking into why two of your grown boys have not registered for the draft."

So that was it! When you don't do what you're supposed to do there are consequences. At this time in history this was the way it was. You had to register for the draft.

The days ahead were long and dreary. Dad and the CPA slaved countless hours over the paper work. There were so many years that were not accounted for that the work never ended. Bonnie, again worked to help answer questions trying to spare mom and dad of the turmoil, plus she helped the CPA straighten out records.

Momma was a wreck and cried all the time. Daddy was frustrated and took his angry temper outs on us kids all the time by yelling and screaming. Life at the Thomas commune was worse than ever. I didn't know anything about Jesus at that time. That if we knew Him He would come to us if we prayed. Unfortunately, I had never had that opportunity since this all occurred before my marriage and the husband that took me to church where I found the "Living Word". When this all came down I would have gone straight to Jesus with my prayer if I'd only known.

Well, no church, no Bible for us. Just keep on living in the Thomas commune and don't talk too much about our lives. I had no friends from school because momma said I had sisters and brothers for friends. The Thomas IRS secret is still a secret to our outside friends. We were threatened if we said anything to anyone. That is commune family life for you. I just knew this household was being put under the knife by the IRS.

God has His plan and things will change one day.

As the thirty days came closer and closer the more afraid we all became. And the government opened up another can of rotten worms.

The government did look into my two brothers and why they had not signed up for the draft.

Dooms day arrived!

The IRS got back with the accountant and looked over the books. They must have felt sorry for dad with ten kids and struck a deal. I guess you could call it a deal. They let dad off with a heavy fine of several thousand dollars, but brought the hammer down on the draft evasion charges against my two brothers.

It all came together. Dad off with fines/ brothers

off to prison.

The scriptures say that God bottles our tears, well I just know he has gallons of mine bottled. That's why I love the verse that says, No more tears, no pain. How glorious that day will be "when we get to heaven."

*Thank you Jesus that because of my taking you as Savior, I am ready for that eternal home. Heaven. I'm Gonna go there!*

In May of 1963... off to prison my two brothers went. They entered Federal prison which happened to be here in Springfield, Missouri so we could at least go visit.

The saddest thing is that the tax accountant told my dad that if he had just filed each year, with all the kids as deductions, he wouldn't have owed anything, in fact he would have received refunds.

When we went to visit our brothers in prison, dad would never go with us. He must have felt miserable knowing it was his actions that put his sons behind bars and cost him a lot of money.

One of the brothers really made the best of it. He got in with the guys, played cards, talked and made the best of a terrible situation. That would be Clyde. I loved him and how sweet he was to us girls.

On the other hand my older brother was miserable. That would be Brother Bill. He stayed alone by himself, never entered into anything, we were so afraid when we went to see him. He always liked my sister Bonnie best and became very dangerous if she mentioned any boy that she was talking to.

Each time we went into see our brothers, usually on Sundays, we were excited to see them, but it also was a very tense time. Same as living in the commune, you might say.

Clyde was always easier to talk to. Bill was so tense and we really couldn't wait to leave the prison facility. He questioned us about everything, I felt like we were on trial because he wasn't at the commune house to check out what we were doing.

How sad for us to have had to live like this. This went on for the entire eighteen months they were there. Finally their release day arrived.

Clyde immediately went back to his former life. Running around to see his old friends and adjusting very well. Bill on the other hand, became very quiet and secluded. He went down to the shop building and began working on projects he had been involved in before his arrest. Bill was very smart. He had invented a ride called the Whirly Bird. Dad got it patented and then they sold all rights to it. It started being built by the new owners and they changed the name to Scrambler.

If you have ever been to any fair or carnival in your life you have ridden this ride that was originally designed by my brother Bill.

It was so unusual, and was the first ride mounted on a trailer. You simply hooked it onto a tractor and drove it to location, unhooked and everything folded out to make the ride complete. You will read how in later chapters how talented Bill was. Even that in his older life he was working on a kiddy ride at age eighty-six.

Before his death in 2015, my deceased brother Clyde said before his death, Bill you will never see that ride finished. That turned out to be true. The last two years of Bill's life became quite a struggle. He began to fall many times. I had become his caregiver the last couple of years, and I am sure many of you reading this can relate.

I know many people have had that role to fill in their lives. Bill was extra hard to be caregiver for. He had a contrary spirit, sort of like what I grew up under--like my tyrant dad.

Since Bill never married, he was not used to anyone trying to assist him and rebelled against everything I tried to do for him. But as this story goes on, you will see that "all things are possible with God." No matter how many times I tried to tell Bill about heaven and his eternity, he never would listen and was very contrary to "the Word".

## CHAPTER FIVE

## God's Plan Can't be Thwarted

God has always had His plan and purpose for each and every one of us. We start out as newborn babies, then progress through living our lives. Then things begin to change for each and every one of us.

My life was no different. I told you earlier in my story how much I wanted to become a singing star. Well, that was not the great plan God had for me. Of course I never understood all this at the time, but as I continue, you will see that God had a much bigger, better plan and purpose for my life.

Being child number seven in a household of ten kids came with many challenges. I didn't realize then what I begin to know later. Even the choice that I made to go to Cosmetology School was all part of God's great plan, because that is where I met my husband after I graduated.

My sister, Bonnie and I had decided to go to cosmetology school and be hairdressers. How hard could it be? We would go, put in our time, graduate and make lots of money! Whoopi! Who would think you had to know about bones, electricity, muscles, and a lot of other things I never dreamed existed. Wasn't it about doing hair? Gee whiz! At that time we even had to do finger waves on the model we took to pass the exam board to obtain our license. Now that's crazy, right?

After we passed that exhausting test, with license in hand, we went to Glen Isle Beauty salon to seek a job. The owner, Jean Evans, really liked us both, but didn't have an opening right then. So as in God's plan, she asked if we would be willing to take evening appointments. We agreed, knowing this would get us started, and it did. So when we were finally on days my life started to change for God's plan,

The owner had a big Christmas party at her home and we all went. It was a fun party, being that I loved to sing, and they had a piano player there, which set it up perfectly for me to sing Rudolf the Red Nosed Reindeer. I put my special cute little spin on the song and I guess I caught the attention of my soon to be husband. Go figure how God works. He took an interest and asked if he could take me home. Since I came with my sister I said yes. We talked a lot all the way home and he seemed to really like me.

We saw each other at the hair salon each day and because he had been through a divorce, and just out of the Navy, I wasn't sure if this is what I really wanted. I still had a hidden desire to be a singing star. What happened there Sarah? We begin to date, which was risky since I was not allowed to leave the commune to date—rules of my tyrant dad.

Then I learned he knew one of my brothers through his brother-in-law. I panicked because I was terrified he would know about my brothers being in prison.

Our dating in 1965.

We only dated six months. That was long enough to know *he* was the one. We eloped, because there was no way I could have a consensual wedding with my family, or should I say father. We planned our trip to be married by a Justice of the Peace in Harrison, Arkansas. For you that have had big beautiful weddings, flowers, bride's maids, and all that goes with it, you would have been in shock at this scene.

Lanty was a kind man, who seemed to care deeply for his parents, and would help out however he could. He had been through two girl relationships that both turned sour, so I suppose I see how he had bad memories of the women in his life.

I suppose because my personality reflected my strict up-bringing in the commune, he thought he had found the girl of his dreams. Except for one thing, we all have our hang-ups and there are always things in our lives that can cause problems. I was one that struggled with my identity. Growing up in such a dysfunctional family in the commune lifestyle, I never really found myself.

And to top it all off, I had never been to church, never heard the gospel word, or that Jesus died for our sins, came to give us eternal life by dying for our sins.

In 1965 I met and fell in love with my now husband of 53 years. You know I couldn't or shouldn't leave the commune so against my families' wishes, Lanty and I eloped and were married on June 13, 1965.

We got things ready, rented an apartment the night before we left for Arkansas, and I smuggled my belongings out of the old home place. My sister Katy was so helpful in helping me by telling me when the coast was clear to get in there and get my stuff.

Funny, not really, but she helped me and I hopefully helped her in leading her to the Lord as her own personal Savior before she took her life in 1974.

Our marriage was so real. Crazy is the word.

We left that Saturday night June 12th for the Justice of the Peace in Arkansas, J.P. Sanders, and arrived at his home by 10:00 p.m. His wife, with curlers in her hair, answered the door.

"Oh, he's out coon hunting, but I can holler for him and he'll come right back."

We waited and he finally arrived then announced, "We have to go down to the lab office and get a blood test in a nonexclusive matter. What?. He takes us in his old pickup truck down a couple of dirt country roads. Lab man?? Didn't know we had to go for lab tests. What other surprises are in store? The lab man meets us there, we get blood test, and I am embarrassed because I had a tight fitting suit jacket on and it was nearly impossible to get my sleeve up to draw blood.

Okay, now that we gave blood and we already had our marriage license. We headed back down the old dirt roads to his home for the ceremony. I guess you could call it that.

Hey, isn't there supposed to be a witness at a marriage? Well Mrs. J.P. Sanders was there but I think she went off to bed since it was after midnight by then. I could not blame her, but I begin to wonder if I should go through with this weird marriage?

J.P. Sanders pronounced our vows, we both said I do, rings were exchanged and we were pronounced Mr. and Mrs. Lanty F. Tyler at 12:45 a.m. Obviously it was to be since at this writing we have been married these 53 years. Who would have ever given this crazy run-away couple, under the circumstances, any chance of success? Goes to show you don't have to have a great big beautiful wedding to make your marriage last, just God and determination.

After a short honeymoon in Eureka Springs, Arkansas, we headed to our little apartment in Springfield, MO. Lanty told me later he was looking in the rear view mirror all the way down to be married and all the way back because he thought there might be hit men sent by my commune family to bump him off.

That sounded funny, but considering my demented family there was a lot of truth in his suspicion. They didn't permit anybody to take us from the commune.

Daddy, being daddy was completely against us, but when Momma died, Lanty went to him and said how sorry he was and how much he would care for me. Daddy just said, "Well, you'll have to prove yourself." That's Daddy.

I know now it was meant to be as you keep reading about this man of my dreams.

Whoa!!!! He was instrumental in my "New life" as a believer in Jesus Christ as savior.

He was the first one to take me to church, where I begin to hear the gospel of Jesus Christ and what Jesus did to redeem us as sinners. Remember, we are all born in sin, because of the fall of Adam and Eve. However, my belief did not come immediately

Lanty & Sarah Tyler today.

## CHAPTER SIX

### *Our Early Marriage Struggles*

Life goes on, I'm in church, and Lanty is the first person to take me. All in God's plan.

### *Looking for a Job*

Lanty traveled to Kansas City to interview for a job. However, when he returned home after his interview there was no job! I was afraid. However I did not know Jesus at that time or I wouldn't have been so afraid. Nothing is impossible with Him.

We decide to go to Rockford, Illinois because Lanty had lived there with his family in years past, It was a place he knew he could find work. Meanwhile I am left behind and oh, yes, pregnant with our first son. Isn't that the way it goes? When things appear to be really rough and your stress level is at its' limit, one more thing is added to try and push you over the edge.

Lanty does get a job and we are able to purchase our first little home--thanks to the VA no money down program back then.

My life there was remarkable and free, something I had never known existed. Then I gave birth to our first son, Farrell. And for the first time in my life, I made a friend since there was no one to stop me. She too had a son, and we took our boys many places together. We enjoyed the times we went to the lake up there in the summer, and took many wonderful walks together. I thought how nice it was to have a friend. It was ironic how Momma and Daddy's deep dark secret robbed me of one of life's greatest gifts—a good friend.

What I am going to share now tells you how our God, I said, *our God*, is so gracious and has His plan. It's my testimony.

I had been struggling with really knowing if I had been truly saved. God needed me to get to where I was because he planned to use me in a special way. We were going to church, I was hearing the word but it was just a lot of words that I did not understand. I was having trouble comprehending, that it's by faith that you are saved. It's not good enough to have that head knowledge and not accept what Jesus did on the cross to take away our sins.

I always wondered, what sins? I have lived a good and faithful life. But that's not why you go to heaven or hell, it's that we all were born in sin, Adam and Eve, remember? *"All have sinned and come short of the glory of God, all have been Born in sin. Romans 3; 23*

So... One evening in July of 1969, I will always remember that year when our first son was two years old, I was reading in 1st John, chapter 5 verses 10-13. My eyes were opened. I saw that without Jesus I am lost, condemned and would not see heaven. Hallelujah, praise God! Now I am ready when I die. Because I accepted Jesus as my savior.

I know you may view this as a repeat, but it's to emphasize "MY TESTIMONY". I remember going to church that next Sunday, going forward in that little Berean Baptist Church. Lanty walked with me and I told Pastor Bro Swanson, that I had trusted Jesus as my Savior. No more just head knowledge... Now He lives within my heart.

I was now 26 years old and our first son was a two year old.       It took our moving to Rockford, Illinois for Gods purpose and plan to unfold in how I was to find the Lord my Savior as in my testimony above.

My husband being a Christian, attending church, hearing the gospel and hearing the plan of salvation many, many , times, it never registered until that night in 1969.

That's just the way God works in a life.  God takes you to another state, puts you with Christians in a GOOD gospel church, listening to messages, and learning Bible scripture to let you finally realize through the working of the Holy Spirit to open your eyes and let you see.

So grateful that I realized my need for Jesus, (the one that died for me) my substitute for my sins. The reason I could finally say: I have eternal life. I am prepared and heaven is my final resting place.

Not that we don't still sin. God knows we are in the flesh and that's why Jesus forgives our present, and future sins. The difference is when you have

Jesus as Savior, you *don't want* to sin.

The Holy Spirit pricks your heart and lets you know that you needed to ask for forgiveness. This is an amazing thing. *That God so loved the world that he sent His only begotten son, that whosoever believeth in him shall not perish but have everlasting life* (John 3:16), and also read John 3-18.

Well, now I am going forward with my new life. You will see I still make mistakes but I have an advocate with the Father to take my battles to Him and He is always there for me. *He will never leave me or forsake me. Hebrews 13:5*

Enters Jesus. *Amazing that God had this plan from the foundation of the world. Because God is a Holy God, we had to have redemption for our sins. All have sinned and come short of the glory of God* (Romans 3: 23-25).

## CHAPTER SEVEN

## *Way, Truth and Life*

This is why, as I repeated in Chapter Six, the importance of my salvation in my story. I can see how God had another one's life plan.

My good friend Connie, that I loved so much, her and her little boy and all the talks, the walks, and laying on the river edge seeing who could get the tannest, was all in God's divine plan. It was later in the year, winter time--burr! Rockford winters, that I received a call from Connie's mother. She said Connie and her husband had been in a bad accident on the icy roads coming back from a New Year's Eve party.

"Connie is paralyzed."

My heart sank and I cried along with Connie's mother. She told me where she was at in the hospital. I made arrangements and went to her hospital room.

I walked in and she was on a gurney type bed where they can turn you over as needed.

Cry, cry, how can this be? I crawled under her

bed so I could talk to her, with my hands and knees on the floor and looking up to Connie, I begin to try and sooth her and comfort her in every possible way I could. I told Connie that nothing is impossible with God! I told her how I had found Jesus as my Savior, and she can have that peace also.

I led her in the salvation message and Connie responded by taking Jesus into her heart and accepting Him as her Savior. I know that didn't heal her, but in a way, yes, it did. Because when you have Jesus when you die you will be totally whole.

I remember coming out of the room and there was a member of the clergy standing there. I told him that Connie just got saved, but he never said a word. He did not even bother to ask how that was possible. He did not even ask how I got that idea, or if I was a believer myself. Stuck in my mind that just because people say they go to church, serve as deacons, sing in church choirs, and serve in so many church areas, even as pastors, ARE YOU WASHED IN THE BLOOD? The soul cleansing blood of the lamb?

Examine your hearts. Be sure you have the saving knowledge that God came to earth in flesh, (Jesus the God man) God with skin on, to redeem your lost soul and make you eternally ready for your glorious home in heaven. So very important to KNOW that you are ready. Make sure!

## CHAPTER EIGHT

*He Never Promised a Rose Garden*

How nice to be back where we call home, Springfield, Missouri in the beautiful Ozarks, filled with hills, valleys, trees, rivers and lakes. We were in Rockford. Illinois for five years. When we moved there remember, I was 6 months pregnant with our first son, Farrell.

I enjoyed those five years living in Rockford. Met my friend that I spoke about in that awful accident and led Connie to the Lord. She is still living but remains paralyzed from the neck down. But you know, because she accepted Jesus as her Savior, the scriptures tell us, she will be totally whole. She will run and jump, Oh. How beautiful for that promise.

When we moved back in 1972 it seemed like all was going so much better, oh, happy days.

As a matter of fact we found a beautiful little A-Frame home nestled right above the Finley River, south of Springfield in Nixa, Missouri. We purchased this home and what a dream it was.

We sold our home in Rockford, Illinois after many dangerous toils and snares. We had a VA loan on it and finally a lady assumed that loan and we were able to move.

Lanty had already taken a new job here in the Springfield area and I was so relieved to get to come back to our roots and join him. Farrell was only five years old and we had to caution him: "DO NOT GO NEAR THE RIVER BELOW" (Finley River) without an adult. He never disobeyed, thank God. We had many happy times in the A-Frame until the tragedy you will read about in the next chapter.

Lord, I know someday I will understand it better by and by. But at this time, I was having more and more problems with unending heartaches.

You are part of my life, *You are my life* at this time and I just thought all would be well.

Not in this old fallen world. They say bad things happen to good people, and the trials and tribulations are just to make us stronger. I should be getting really strong at this point in my life but as you will see in the chapters to follow, things get worse and worse.

I cry unto the Lord: Lord have mercy on my soul. But even in the valley you are there. I had mountain top experiences and then deep, deep valley experience.

This next chapter was a real test of my faith. Katy sister number eight, right in my home that I opened to her, tried to help in her misery, tried to give her guidance, but so thankful as you will read, led her soul to Jesus.

## CHAPTER NINE

From the Novella

*In Loving Memory of Katy. One of Ten Thomas children*

SUICIDE is dedicated to all who have gone through the terrible nightmare, as I have, of a loved one taking their own life. To all whom think they might see signs and warnings from a loved one you have concerns about, this story is to help you see the action you must take.

I would like to give to you what I found to be true. In that I, and perhaps you, have always had a question on suicide. What is the fate of a loved one and their destiny if they choose suicide? This story about my sister Katy, not only lets you feel and share my emotions as I reveal them to you, but it also shows you the *awesome power* of our Great and Mighty Savior, Jesus Christ.

I've found that He is waiting with open arms to welcome *whosoever may come*. When we belong to Him nothing shall separate us from the love of God.

May this real suicide story let you cry, scream, get angry and maybe even smile, right along with me. I hope it helps put to rest any doubts you might have concerning suicide, and the fate of your loved one.

## SUICIDE CHAPTER 1

On that cold and windy day in March of 1974, I was so very tired. After a day trip to Joplin, Lanty and I were driving to our home on the Finely River. He'd just taken a new job, and the crew in the office wanted to meet me. It had been a nerve-wracking day, and little did I know, it was about to get worse...but let me start at the beginning of this tragic story.

In the fall of 1973 I went to visit my younger sister Katy in Florida. Katy was the eighth child in a family of ten. It was the first time I'd gone to see her there, and the first time I met her new husband. I also got acquainted with his two children from his previous marriage, who lived with them.

During my time at their house, I realized Katy wasn't in an ideal marriage. Matter of fact, she seemed pretty unhappy to me. The man was controlling and demanding. I knew by my sister's actions she was somewhat afraid of him. However, I didn't think it was my place to butt into their affairs.

One day while I was there, Katy wanted to take me shopping. We went to this big mall because her husband wanted her to get him a new briefcase. I, as usual, looked for the best buys. I showed her one I found that wasn't cheap, but wasn't the top of the line.

"Oh, no," she said. "He won't settle for that. It has to be very expensive."

The look on her face told me she was afraid she couldn't please him. Needless to say, I didn't make any more suggestions, I just let her get what she thought was the right one. Apparently she did, I didn't hear him complain.

When it was time for me to return to Missouri, I left her behind with a man and a situation I felt uneasy about. Even though they got along good at times, I knew my sister, and she wouldn't have wanted me to worry, so she pretended things were okay.

Nevertheless I could tell she was depressed and that worried me. You see, I had good reason to feel anxious, because I knew she was capable of harming herself. She'd already made several unsuccessful attempts to take her own life.

One time she took a half bottle of aspirin at a friend's house. On another occasion she cut her wrist, and on one occasion she tried to gas herself. Thankfully, she had called someone each time and we were able to save her.

I just prayed those times were behind her. After I got home we talked now and again on the phone. Though I never asked, she sounded as if all was going well, so that helped me calm my fears, and I went on with less anxiety about her situation.

Days turned into weeks, weeks to months, the holidays were over, and thank goodness, spring was just around the corner. Katy and I continued to talk; we didn't get into deep conversation, just light-hearted sister type of talking.

Then one day, she called and told me she was leaving her husband. She said she was going to Springfield to stay with one of her old friends for a while. I knew the friend she spoke about, and thought it would probably be a good place for her to be. I was actually relieved that she had finally left him.

A few days after Katy arrived in Springfield, I received a phone call that started a very unsettling time for me. When I answered Katy was on the line, and she spoke to me in a disturbingly urgent voice. I was familiar with every one of her voices and moods, but I had never heard this kind of emotion from her before.

"I need to come to your house. Can you come and get me?"

I glanced at the clock over the fireplace mantel and it read 3:30. Lanty was still at work, Farrell, now seven years old, was playing at a friend's house, and there was a terrible snow storm outside. How could I leave my child and run off in this weather? Especially since we lived more than few miles away from where she was. "Oh, Katy, it's so bad out. I don't think I can make it there." I felt bad because I knew from her tone she was very upset about something.

I tried to calm her. "You'll be okay. Just settle down and let's talk. Maybe when Lanty gets home we can both come and get you.

"No! I need to come to your house now!"

She sounded so desperate. The pleading in her voice tore at my heart and I realized I couldn't turn her down. "Okay, I'm on my way." The line went silent. She hung up on me. I placed the receiver back into the cradle, and set out on my mission.

I got my coat and went to my 4x4 Jeep. The snow was blinding and I was scared to drive in weather like this by myself, but I kept driving. I made it over some of the biggest snow drifts I'd seen in a long time. Then I reached one of the steep Ozark hills and tried to get up it, but the vehicle couldn't make it. I wondered who said a Jeep could go anywhere? It was clear to they were wrong because this mean 4x4 just could not handle this big March snow storm with icy hills.

I'd only gotten about two miles from home when, with a heavy heart, I decided to turn back. I figured I'd just call her when I got home, and prayed she would understand.

After almost slipping off the road twice, I finally arrived back to my warm, inviting home. The cozy fire, in the huge fireplace, welcomed me while I removed my snow covered wraps and sat down to call Katy.

The phone line buzzed with each ring, and when she answered I blurted, "I couldn't make it. I tried, Katy. I really did. I'm so sorry. We can just talk by phone."

Katy sobbed. "I have to get to your house now!"

No matter how hard I tried to reason with her, she wouldn't listen. Finally I said, "Okay, how about if you call a taxi cab. I'll pay half of the cost." I felt so bad to think I was so cheap I would say that, but was not surprised when she took me up on my offer.

"Okay. I'm calling the cab the second I hang up. I'll be there soon."

I sat by the fire and waited. It was a good hour before my phone rang again. On the other end was Katy.

"Sarah I think I am lost. I'm somewhere in Rogersville. I don't know where. The taxi driver let me off in front of this house and it is not your house. I told him it's not the right place. But when he asked me where it was, I couldn't tell him. So, he stopped so I could call you to see how to get there."

By this time I was pretty upset. How on earth had she gotten to Rogersville? "Katy, go back to your friend's house in Springfield."

"No, I just can't."

"Then let me talk to the taxi driver." She put him on the phone and I told him how to get to my home on the Finley River.

He said, "Well we're in a totally different direction. It'll take a while, but we will head that way."

It was a good two hours later when, out the picture window, I saw Katy trudging through the deep snow. I opened the door and let the poor, snow covered, lost child into my house. I helped her remove her wet coat and scarf. Her shoes were soaked through and through, she had to have been in the snow for a while. "Where did you walk from?"

When she didn't answer, it was obvious she was tired, worn, and confused. She needed time to settle down so I walked her to the end of the couch closest to the fire and helped her settle on the cushions. After what seemed like forever, I couldn't take anymore. "Katy, say something. Scream or whatever, just talk to me."

I sat motionless waiting, almost afraid. She finally started crying. I moved to the couch, sat next to her, pulled her close and just held her tight until she was ready. Her despair seeped into me and I somehow sensed she had never been this down before.

"I was so lost."

My heart went out to her, because I felt there was more to her condition than she realized. I began to talk about the Lord Jesus and how He loves us so much, and how He came to die for our sins. I'd told her this before but never thought she understood.

I think most of our family always knew about God. *But then even the devil believes in God and trembles. 1, James 2:19* Most of our family never made it into church, or under the word of God. Lanty was the reason I did. He was the first to take me to church, where I really had the opportunity to hear the plan of salvation. I responded to God's word in 1969 and was saved. Praise the Lord.

I began to tell Katy, "*Jesus is the way, the truth, and the life. No one comes to the father except through the Son, Jesus.*" *2. John 14:6*. I told her how Jesus wanted to be her savior, to forgive her of all her sins. Through her tears she looked up at me.

" I have done too many bad things. He will never forgive me."

"We are all sinners; we were born in sin, that's why *God sent His only son Jesus, to die in our place.*" *John 3:16.* "When we trust Him as our savior He gives us eternal life." I tried to stress to her the supreme power of our Savior. "Believe in the Lord Jesus Christ. Ask Him to forgive you for your sins, and you will be saved. Forever and ever, you'll spend eternity with Him."

"I want that, I need that peace. I am so lost."

Oh, how my heart jumped with joy just knowing she wanted to be saved. "Katy, we can do that right now. Do you want to ask Him?"

When she nodded, I took her hand, and she and I got down by the fireplace hearth. We knelt, bowed our heads and I told her, "Just ask Jesus to come into your heart. Ask him to forgive you of all sins."

Quiet filled the room and I began to pray silently, *"Oh father, please help her to know you and your great love and forgiveness, please help her."*

Katy started to cry again. "I'm too bad!"

I knew Satan was trying hard to stop her from the sinner's prayer, just like he tried to keep her from getting to my house. I refused to let him get in the way of this moment. "Are you saying God is not big enough to forgive you? Do you believe He sent Jesus to die in your place?" It was silent for a few moments, and then it happened!

She began to call out, "Please forgive me Jesus for all my sins. Please help me and come into my heart. I believe and trust in *You*."

I know bells weren't ringing, or maybe they were, but I felt, right then*, that heaven and the angels were rejoicing for this little lost sheep that now was a "found sheep." 4. Luke 15:10.* I knew from scripture that Katy was now a child of the King. Forever and ever, no matter what.

Tears streamed down her cheeks, and when she lifted her head I held her hand tightly. "Now, if you were to die tonight, where would your soul be?"

Smiling, Katy answered, "In heaven, because I

prayed and trusted Jesus as my Savior."

After our experience that evening, and during the week following, my younger sister seemed to be doing so much better. I felt like all was going to be good now, and I would never have to worry again about her being depressed.

We talked about many things in the days to come. Since she was going through a divorce, I thought a new direction in her life would be good for her, so I mentioned she might join the military. She perked up at the suggestion and agreed it was a good idea. We made a plan to start toward her new goal at the beginning of the next week.

Katy was such a beautiful girl, only twenty-seven years old. Her secret dream was to become a professional ballet dancer. She had taken countless lessons and was such a graceful dancer. I was heartsick for her because I also shared the loss of a personal dream, but maybe now she would find the help and direction she needed to turn her life around.

## SUICIDE CHAPTER 2

Friday came and I was really looking forward to the weekend. That day, Katy agreed to stay with Farrell so I could go with my husband to his new Joplin office.

This was the cold, windy March day in 1974. Lanty and I left early because Katy was going to get Farrell off to school. She was also going to be there when he got home. I trusted her completely with my child.

About three o'clock that afternoon, I thought about phoning home to see how things were going. Something compelled me to make the call, but when I looked at the new, elaborate, multi-lined phone system, I was intimidated. The last thing Lanty needed was for me to break something.

I let the notion fall to the wayside. Besides, Katy really didn't have that much to do; I figured she'd had a nice relaxing day, home alone, waiting for Farrell. I had already made our supper, of spaghetti and garlic bread, all Katy had to do was put it on to warm around 6:00 pm. That's about the time we figured we'd get back from Joplin.

All was planned. Or was it?

Lanty and I pulled into the carport of our home. I breathed a sigh of relief to be back at my safe haven. Then, as I walked from the carport to the front door, an eerie feeling came over me. The sound of the chimes on the front porch, cling-cling-clinging, was almost deafening, and the howling March wind literally scooted me along. I opened the front door as fast as I could and shot inside. My chimes usually sounded beautiful to me, but that day, the ringing cut through me like a knife.

My son was on the couch all involved in his after school cartoons. "Hi, Farrell, where's Aunt Katy?"

He shrugged. "Upstairs maybe. Changing her clothes. I haven't seen her."

I didn't mean to yell, but fear flew through me, and it just came out. "You mean you haven't seen her since you been home from school?" His timid answer told me my reaction really frightened him. I was afraid. No terrified of what Katy might have done, and why he hadn't seen her.

"No, Mom."

In a mad dash I flew up the stairs to the bedroom Katy had been staying in. With my hand on the doorknob, I called out to my heavenly Father, "O God please, no, don't let what I am thinking be true. Let her be resting. Let her just be reading. Just let her be okay"

I pounded on the bedroom door, and hollered, "Katy, Katy, please open the door, please let me in!" She didn't answer. "Katy, please!" Pound, pound, pound. "Please, oh God, please, Katy, let me in!"

My plea was answered with silence. I thought my heart was going to beat out of my chest as my world came crushing in on me. I turned and started back down the stairs, when I met Lanty running up to me. His face was riddled with worry.

"Sarah, what's wrong?"

"I just know she has done something awful. I can't take this." I know my husband well. He was aware of her problems and was thinking the same thing. "Oh, Lanty, please don't let this be what we think."

He turned and I knew where he was going. To check the guns. I followed close behind to see if they were where they were supposed to be. We had a huge lodge-type fireplace where we kept a shotgun and a twenty-two rifle standing up in the corner of the hearth.

It took scant seconds for us to reach the fireplace. The rifle was gone! At that moment, my heart broke and a blast of emotions ran through me. I knew if she had that gun, it was too late. Too Late! I couldn't stop trembling and tears rushed down my face in a stormy truant. Time stood still until I heard Lanty's voice.

"I can't do this alone. I'm going to call Bob for help."

I don't think I said anything, but I knew Bob would be a good person to assist. He was one of those neighbors everyone needs. He'd be there for you through thick or thin.

While we waited, I didn't know what to do. Everything was moving so fast, but at the same time it happened in slow motion. Nothing around me felt real. All I could do is hold on to the hope that maybe she wasn't dead, that she'd only injured herself and would fully recover. In my heart, I knew that wasn't the case, but what do you do without hope?

We lived in a rural area, and our homes were too far apart for Bob to walk. Then I heard his car come screeching into the driveway and he ran inside. I listened while they made a plan as to what to do.

They decided to put a tall ladder up to the dormer window of the bedroom where Katy was staying. Lanty climbed up while Bob held it steady. They did this in case she was lying in bed contemplating using the gun on herself. If that was the case, they could stop her.

To say I was scared to death standing there at the bottom of that ladder would be a huge understatement. I closed my eyes, forced myself to breathe and prayed, *Oh, my father, please, this can't be. I can never go on. I don't want to go on. Why would you let something like this happen? Wasn't all well with her when we had our talk a few days ago"*

Lanty's footsteps stopped at the top of the ladder. I was waiting almost afraid to open my eyes, but I did and looked up at my husband. His face was pale when he met my gaze

"She did it."

"No!" I whispered, or screamed, I really don't know for sure. All I knew was that I felt completely broken. My heart and my life shattered right there in the cold winter wind. I began to shake. I could hardly stand while I waited for Lanty to do, or say something. I tried to breathe but the air barely seeped into my body.

"Suicide."

Such an ugly word. Suicide. I didn't know it then, but the word would hold me in its grips for years to come. The moment he said suicide my heart dropped to my feet. It couldn't have happened. I just wanted to get away from the ugliness. Go.

Run as fast as I could to stop the reality of what was happening. "No! No, no!"

I only managed to run few feet before I fell flat on the ground. I screamed and rolled into a fetal position. I didn't want to be alive. This nightmare could not be real because I didn't want to live the reality of what my sister had done.

"Why? Why?" I cried, still wallowing on the cold, hard ground. "Katy, why did you do this? Why did you hurt us like this?" I'd never felt like this before. Such raw emotions, anger, fear, disgust, hurt and lost love. A sister, so dear to me, gone. None of which I could even begin to control. Yes, the reality of life hit me straight on. My world changed that instant, the twenty-ninth day of March, nineteen seventy-four.

Lanty came off the ladder and picked Sarah up. "Sarah, you need to come in and be with Farrell. He's crying and very upset because you're so hurt."

Of course I needed to go to my son, who I knew desperately needed help. I felt so bad. I was a wreck. How could I comfort my son when I needed comforting myself? I fought hard to bring myself under control and managed to stand. After a few moments in Lanty's arms, and a several reassuring looks from him, I forced myself to go back into the house.

So many things had to be done. Other family members needed to be notified, but I just couldn't function. Thank God for Lanty and Bob. They called the sheriff and my family, while I lay on the sofa, my head pounding, my stomach aching, and little Farrell standing over me.

"Mom, it will be okay."

The poor thing was so worried and confused. I hugged his neck and tried to comfort him the best I could while still on my own emotional rollercoaster. From my place on the couch, out the picture window, I watched the Christian County sheriff pull into the drive. Right behind him was a deputy and an ambulance. Then I heard someone say there were TV reporters. It was all too much for me to comprehend.

TV reporters? Absolutely not! I wasn't going to have them prying into our private lives. My poor sister lay dead upstairs by her own hand! Didn't they know we were heartbroken? I cried out to someone, anyone who'd listen. "Tell those reporters to leave! I don't want them here!" I saw the deputy go outside and tell them to leave. I breathed a sigh of relief when they drove away without their *story*.

My husband and Bob were in the process of taking the bedroom door off, but they didn't go inside the room. They knew the authorities wouldn't want anything touched before they got there. The sheriff came in and made his way up to the bedroom, while I remained on the sofa, unable to move a muscle.

Family members who lived locally began to arrive. Some lived out of state and wouldn't be able get there until the day of the funeral. The house was full of people when the sheriff came down the stairs and made his way into the living room. He explained how he had looked for any evidence that could explain what exactly happened. Various scenarios were tossed around. Like, could someone have come in and killed her? Was it a robbery gone wrong? There were many more, but of course, it was none of those things.

"I need to ask you some questions, ma'am."

It took every ounce of what little strength I had left to sit up, but I managed. I watched the ambulance drivers make their way upstairs to get Katy's small, frail body. They would then bring her down and take to the morgue. That was something I did not want to see or think about.

"Mrs. Tyler, was there a suicide note?"

"I don't know." I vaguely remember standing up and walking to the breakfast bar area. "I didn't look." I glanced everywhere she may have left a note, but saw nothing so I went back to the sofa and sat down. The sheriff was busy writing something in his tablet.

"Was she depressed about anything?"

All of Katy's problems ran through my mind. "Yes." I began to tell him Katy's story, including her failed attempts to hurt herself before. The reasons for those attempts were difficult for me to recount, but I did tell him about her bad marriage, a miscarriage and countless other problems she had that seemed to go on and on.

After asking all the questions he could think of, the sheriff walked away and I lay back down. The sound of the paramedics making their way downstairs with Katy was more than I could bear. I could not watch them take her lifeless body out of my house. I covered my face and held my eyes shut as tightly as humanly possible. The door opened and the sounds echoed in my mind while they took her away and closed the door behind them. I waited until I heard the engine of the ambulance and the sound of them leaving the driveway. Did I dare open my eyes?

Then I heard the sheriff talking to my family. I didn't want to listen, but it couldn't be helped. They were so close.

"I looked for bullets in the room, but didn't find any lodged in the walls or anywhere else. In some suicide attempts, the person will test fire the gun before they actually shoot themselves. In some cases the gun will jam and that's why some aren't successful. Unfortunately in this case she was not that lucky. The ones who really want to die will succeed. They find a way, no matter what."

Did he have to keep talking? I wanted to put my hands over my ears and block every painful explanation that came out of his mouth. Didn't he know how agonizing this was? But he just kept talking and talking....

"I know this will be hard to hear, but I figure, as her family members, you would want to know exactly what happened to your loved one." He cleared his throat. "She lay down on the bed, and positioned the rifle parallel to her body. She then placed the tip of the barrel under her chin and pulled the trigger."

"Oh, no!" I cried and held my head. "Oh, why? Why? Why?" I was so afraid my family would all think was my fault. Would they think since she'd been at my house I should have known she was having these thoughts? Maybe they'd wonder why I left her alone if I knew she was unstable. Why didn't I get her help? Was it because she seemed better and I just didn't think it would ever come to this?

No. My family couldn't possibly blame me. They knew Katy had tried this before. They probably had asked themselves some of those same questions. Why did my thoughts always condemn *me*? Why did I always feel responsible for everyone and everything?

I started thinking about what Bonnie had told me a few months earlier. She said Katy had called her and said her husband wanted them to become 'swingers.' I didn't really know what that was, so Bonnie explained to me how couples would get together and changed partners to have sex. I couldn't believe the man she married would ever suggest such a thing.

Then she went on to say he wanted Katy to buy sexual apparatus and have sex with herself in front of him. How dare he put her through that! I jumped up off the couch, my head pounding with the fury I felt at that moment. Through all the commotion, I sprinted to the phone and called that lousy husband of hers. I couldn't stop myself. All I could think of was that this was his fault!

When he answered, I yelled into the receiver, "I hope you're happy now! I hope you'll see how *you* caused this!" I saw one of my sisters running toward me.

"Sarah! This will do no good now. It will just upset all of us even more. Let it go."

She was right. Pointing an accusing finger wouldn't bring Katy back. I was blinded by everything that had happened, and my emotions were running wild. I had to get control of myself. I put the phone down, took a deep breath and worked hard to pull myself together. Being strong right now was totally out of my reach. I was a wreck and there was so much to be done.

Everyone knew there were arrangements to be made, but like me, no one was up to it, so we decided to wait until the next day. I was exhausted and my family realized my condition.

Finally, one by one they left. Now the house was quiet, too quiet. There was no way I could sleep a wink if we stayed here. Lanty, dear Lanty comforted me as best he could. Then he suggested we go to his parents' house for the night, I agreed without a further thought.

By the time we got there I was running on empty. Lanty led me into the house, and told his mother that Katy had committed suicide. There was that word…again.

Truthfully, I don't remember much of anything about that evening. I don't even know if Farrell went with us, I do know, however, my father-in-law gave me something to help me sleep. The much needed rest was welcomed.

\* \* \*

Bonnie, Lanty and I walked into our pastor's office on Saturday. Since he had never met Katy, Pastor Neidy required some details of her life so he could work on the service. He was happy to hear that only a week before, she had trusted Jesus and taken Him as her savior. He listened while we told him about her miscarriage and her unhappy life.

"She was so new in Christ," Pastor said, "She didn't have time to know how God could help her with the battles she faced."

"That is so true," I agreed. "She was really confused, and in my heart I feel that after she accepted the Lord, Satan most likely came to her and made her believe she was still hopeless and discouraged her again."

Pastor Neidy nodded. "You're probably right."

I wiped a tear from my cheek. "*Well, he is a liar*" (5. John 8:44).

Lanty led the way out of the church. Everyone was gathered to talk about Katy and write her obituary. It was hard but it had to be done, and at the same time we were able to reminisce and discuss what Katy had meant in each our lives.

We spoke of how much we loved her, and how her dreams would never be fulfilled. We talked about the sorrow in our hearts that we didn't take the actions we could have to help her through her depression. We wondered why we didn't acknowledge that her marriage was completely wrong, and why none of us tried to get Katy out of that situation before it came to this.

We had all seen little, *and* big warning signs along the way. However, like most families, we were busy with our own lives, and we were afraid that if we were wrong, we would ruin Katy's life. It was just easier to let those subtle warning signs go un-noticed. The honest discussion we had brought is closer to each other in many ways.

The next morning I found myself at church. It had only been two days, but that was the place I most wanted to be. I always knew that *in God's word* was where I would find hope to battle this tragedy. *He is a very present help in time of need* (6. Psalm 46:1).

The day of Katy's funeral arrived. Our friends and family congregated to celebrate her life, and the pastor's message was so fitting. He used the bible passage in John 11:1-44, where Mary and Martha had lost their brother in death. He told the bible story how Jesus was a friend to that family and when he came to them after Lazarus died. Jesus wept. (John 11:35)

Pastor Neidy said, "If we could do as Jesus did in this story, in the scriptures when He called Lazarus from the grave, we could call, "Katy! Come forth!" She would not want to come back. Not from where she is now. Heaven is her resting place.

"She no longer has the pains and hurts of life. She is forever in the arms of her Lord and savior. Katy made her provisions for this glorious land by trusting in Jesus as her lord and savior prior to her quick departure.

"As witnessed, by her sister Sarah, she called on Jesus." (7. Romans 10:13).

He continued to say, "The Lord knows those that are His, and He knows those that need to *come home* from their struggles. God wanted to bring Katy home to safety and into His loving arms, where she would forever be loved and taken care of."

The pastor stopped speaking and our wonderful

friend, Karen (the wife of the music minister) sang a song that I will never forget. She sang the very words I had told Katy that snowy March day while she and I kneeled to ask Jesus into her heart.

She crooned, "He is the way, without Him there's no going. He is the truth, without Him there's no knowing. He is the life, now and forever. He satisfies the longing heart and fills us with His love so rich and free," (2. John 14:6).

I knew, as I sat there in the funeral service, that my sister was with Jesus. I had that 'blessed hope'. Katy didn't have time to find out that Jesus would have satisfied her longing heart and fill her with His love so rich and free. But she knew Jesus had forgiven her of all her sins, because she had trusted Him as her Savior.

## SUICIDE CHAPTER 3

I need to tell you that life became very hard for me in the days to come. I was tested many times in my Christian walk, but I continued to pray. Terrible nightmares riddled my sleep. Loneliness bogged me down, and I allowed my imagination to run away with me. I was so afraid when I was home by myself.

For instance, like a lot of us did, I used to wash my hair in the kitchen sink. It was a normal thing. However, I had to stop doing it.

After Katy's death, when I would have my head turned down in the sink, my eyes closed to keep the soap out, I would hear things. It would sound as if someone was walking upstairs. Then I would hear voices. I felt as if someone was standing directly behind me. I'd begin to cry. I would have to bring my head up and open my eyes to reassure myself.

There were other scary times as well. About two weeks after Katy's funeral, I was going through some papers and something caught my eye. It was Katy's handwriting. Immediately, I thought it might be a suicide note. When I picked up the piece of paper my heart was beating so hard. Then I began to read.

*To Whom It May Concern: My sister Sarah has permission to get into my safety box.*

It went on to give the name of the bank, the box number, etc. I went to the location and gained access to the safe deposit box. There was only one item inside, her wedding ring.

Was this her equivalent to a note? Was there a meaning to the item she left behind? Was it telling me her failed marriage was why she took her life? I can always assume, but I won't truly know the answers to these questions until the day I meet my sister in heaven.

Remember the chimes that were on my front porch? I had to take them down. They seemed to ring and cling at the strangest times. Unfortunately that ringing sound reminded me of that awful day that my sister ended her life. Some memories are best forgotten.

With all the sounds I kept thinking I heard upstairs, I didn't like to go up there. However, I had to because that's where Lanty's and my bedroom was located. It came to the point where I hated to pass the spare bedroom where she took her life. No matter how much cleaning had been done, nothing could ever erase the horrible tragedy that happened within those walls.

We put our house up for sale, but it didn't sell. We had little choice, so we took it off the market. Then, Lanty came up with a good idea to help me with my worst fears.

"What if we take the floor out of that room? It would open up the view to the lower living room. It wouldn't be a room at all, more like a view below, like a loft."

No walls. I could just walk past to our bedroom. "I wouldn't have to see that awful room again?"

"Nope." Lanty smiled.

"I love that idea!"

We began the remodeling project. Everything

went fairly smooth. Then one day, while we were tearing out a wall behind where the bed had been, we made a discovery. A bullet.

Then I knew she probably fired the gun once before she actually executed the round that killed her. This was just as the sheriff had said happens in a lot of suicide cases.

Now I wonder if Katy fired the first bullet to see if the rifle worked? Did she want to see which angle she needed to lay the rifle properly to make sure it completed her intentions?

I wrestled with those thoughts and struggled with the fact the coroner put the time of death at about 3:00 p.m. That's the exact time I thought to call home that day. What if I had made that phone call from Lanty's office in Joplin? If I wouldn't have been afraid to use the multi-line phone system, would I have interrupted her? Maybe stopped her? Would she have even answered?

I will never know the answers until I see Katy again. Oh, yes, I believe I will see her again. I believe that because *the dead in Christ shall rise first and we that remain shall be caught up to meet them in the air. And forever we shall be with The Lord* (1.Thessalonians 4:16-17).

\* \* \*

Life goes on as it always does. Many snowy, windy days have come and gone since that life-changing day. My family paraded on. Lanty and I gave Farrell, who was turning fifteen years old, a baby brother November 3, 1981. That was pretty special for Farrell. Our Travis gave his older brother someone to guard and protect as they both matured.

Farrell grew up, went to college in St. Louis, graduated with a Bachelor of Science Degree and is a well-adjusted man. He is married now, and has a great job. We are proud of him, and happy he is living his life to the fullest.

Lanty truly became my very best friend. He always let me talk about that earth-shaking event. He completely understood how much it affected us both, and he was always there to let me cry and vent my frustrations. Still, to this day, he listens when I need an ear and comforts me when I need an embrace. He is a true blessing.

I've had many occasions to witness to others about this same tragedy in their lives. I've assured them that, if their loved one knew Jesus as their savior, then there's no doubt that their loved one, even though they couldn't handle the pressures and took their own life, is in the arms of Jesus. *If they believed in Him, they will live eternally in heaven* (3. John 3:16).

I am able to say that in writing this story of my experience with suicide, I have learned, and been comforted by, the knowledge of all I have come to realize. To all who will read this, remember, none of us knows what took place in the final fleeting moments of your loved one. You don't know if somewhere along the way your loved one heard a salvation message, but didn't respond at that time. However, they could have done so later, before they took their life.

In growing my knowledge of the scriptures, I

have found that Jesus sticks closer than a brother. His word is so true.

There was a reason Katy never succeeded in any of the other times she attempted to take her life. I know now, she wasn't ready to meet the Lord and savior of her life, and I am so thankful to have been there to witness her salvation. The greatest life-changing event she experienced. *To see her calling on Jesus to save her because that's what made her ready* (7. Romans 10:13).

I'd like to offer comfort and peace to those of you who are struggling with the heartbreaking fact of suicide. It is a fact. *However, it's also a fact that nothing can separate us from the love of Jesus* (9. Romans 8:38-39). I know you must have faith in the bible to know, believe and understand this fact.

Please, read the scriptures, for in them you have life. In the Word of God you will see how trusting Jesus as your savior, is the one fact that makes you, or your loved one, ready to meet The Lord.

And in offering advice, I need to say. If you think you see areas in your loved ones life that needs your intervention, then please, do not be afraid to intervene.

I see now where I, *we*, our family, and friends should have done something on Katy's behalf. I can offer you this true account, *you* might make the difference in that loved ones life. Seek professional help, pursue counseling, listen to them and don't pass it off when they say things like, *I want to kill myself.* That, in its own way, is their cry for help.

Two years ago God gave me a *second* chance to keep this tragedy from happening in our family again. Another sister, the tenth one of the Thomas kids, was at the same point in her life as Katy had been.

We saw, we heard, and we said… *No! Not again.* So, this time my sister Bonnie and I took the situation into our own hands, and of course God's. It was the hardest thing we ever had to do, but we took legal action and had her locked in a facility so she could be helped. That in itself is another story, but to give you the good ending, she is well and adjusted today.

Oh! There is one more thing I'd love to shout out in this suicide story. I'm so excited to let you know that I learned, later in the scriptures, that I actually had angels in my home on the Finley River on March 29, 1974.

I know angels come to carry the soul of the child of God to heaven when they die. I've heard in many instances where before a person passes, they see angels. Sometimes on the foot of their bed, sometimes surrounding them, you can't limit the ways angels appear before they carry the soul away, but it happens. I'm sure of it. (10. Luke 16:22). Now, that's exciting!

For some time, when I would go over the hill then cross the Finely River, I would think, *Katy's not here to enjoy any of this.* Well, I don't live on the Finley River anymore and now I realize, she's enjoying much more than me. She's in Heaven with the Lord.

## * Verses from the King James Version:

James 2:19: Thou believest that there is one God; thou doest well: the devils also believe, and tremble.

John 14:6: Jesus saith unto him, I am the way, the truth, and the life: no man cometh unto the Father, but by me.

John 3:16: For God so loved the world, that he gave his only begotten Son, that whosoever believeth in him should not perish, but have everlasting life.

Luke 15:10: Likewise, I say unto you, there is joy in the presence of the angels of God over one sinner that repentant.

John 8:44: Ye are of your father the devil, and the lusts of your father ye will do. He was a murderer from the beginning, and abode not in the truth, because there is no truth in him. When he speaketh a lie, he speaketh of his own: for he is a liar, and the father of it.

Psalms 46: 1: God is our refuge and strength, a very present help in trouble.

Romans 10:13: For whosoever shall call upon the name of the Lord shall be saved.

1 Thessalonians 4:16-17: [16]For the Lord himself shall descend from heaven with a shout, with the voice of the archangel, and with the trump of God: and the dead in Christ shall rise first: [17]Then we which are alive and remain shall be caught up together with them in the clouds, to meet the Lord in the air: and so shall we ever be with the Lord.

Romans 8:38-39: [38] For I am persuaded that neither death nor life, nor angels nor principalities nor powers, nor things present nor things to come, [39] nor height nor depth, nor any other created thing, shall be able to separate us from the love of God which is in Christ Jesus our Lord.

Luke 16:22a: And it came to pass, that the beggar died, and was carried by the angels into Abraham's bosom.

## CHAPTER TEN

*Life Moves on – More Heartaches and Tears*

When Mommy died in 1964 and then my daddy in 1968, we as the Thomas clan, decided to let Bill stay and live in the old home place. He had lived there since we all moved there in 1952. He wasn't married so he lived alone. We never dreamed he would still be living there at age 86, which meant we could not sell the home.

In 2013 my sister Bonnie and her husband decided to turn Bill over to me for the paying of his bills, taking him to doctor appointments, and any and all things that he needed done. He didn't get along with my brother-in-law, and since Bonnie was in the beginning stages of Alzheimer's, I had to come into play. My work started, and being a caregiver turned out to be much harder than I ever dreamed possible.

*Lord, how will I ever get through this? How will I understand the things that I will be called upon to take care of? Only through Your help and guidance will I see my way clear.*

I turned to this particular chapter and verses in Psalms 108: 12-13. This passage became my anchor. It would hold me through much turmoil as I proceeded through my brother Bill's sickness, trust situations, and all that lay ahead.

So many things came up over the two years that I had this responsibility. I discovered a gas leak smell, and had to call the gas company to come out and find the leak. They fixed the leak in the ground and all seemed well. Then later there was a water leak underground which cost $12,000 to repair.

One Monday in April the plumbers call my cell phone to say they need into house to install a new electric hot water heater. They tell me they can't reach Bill. "Can you call and see how we can get in?

Well, call, call, and call, no answer from Bill. So I decide to run on over to the house. I unlock the front door and go from room to room calling his name. No Bill. His truck was at the house and he always drives it even down to the shop building if he was down there.

I ran down to shop. No Bill. I go back to the house, calling his name again. The only place I had not looked was upstairs, but he never went up there. Bill only lived on the first floor level. So up the stairs I go calling his name.

Once on the second floor I see the door to the attic open and the skinny, wooden ladder hanging down. I call up the steps, Bill, Bill. I finally hear a faint voice say, "Yes help!" I hurry up the shaky stairs into the dark. I can't see him anywhere. He says follow over by the flashlight. I look under an old stored table and there he is flat on his back. He yells, "Get me out!"

"Bill there's no way I can lift you!" He wanted me to drag him out using the old dirty blanket he was lying on top of like a dead man.

*Lord, how can I begin to get him out from under that old table? I'm too small and he's too heavy.* He kept saying, "you can do it!"

I grabbed the ends of that raggedy old blanked and pulled. He moved about six inches. I pulled harder. It took everything I had, but I managed to drag the blanket to an area clear enough that I might be able to sit him up. I desperately wanted to call the Emergency people, but Bill kept yelling at me to do it myself. He just kept saying I could do it.

I took one deep breath. "Here we go. You'll have to put your one hand on that table and give me the other hand, On the count of three I'll lift. One, two, three!" Can you believe he came up and immediately moved to the steps and started down. He said he needed water. Once I saw him in the light it was obvious he was very dehydrated. Once I got down and talked with him I learned he'd fallen a day and half ago. No water and no necessary medication. God had His plan.

Okay. This is one recovery. Next one was only a few weeks later when he fell getting out of his truck down at the shop. It was cold, windy and no one was around. Here comes the plan of God again.

Grace, Grace, God's Grace. He has His plan.

He had drug himself over to get into some fallen leaves and was lying there when, as only God can ordain, an old friend he knew came driving up to his shop. He said he saw something curled up in the leaves and thought it was some old bum who needed help. He discovered it was Bill.

He managed to get Bill to his feet and helped him into shop to warm him up. That was the number two rescue in a short period of time.

*God thank you for keeping him alive as we look to the next time that it becomes more serious! Grace, Grace, Wonderful Grace. How great thou Are.*

It is second day of July, my birthday. I had a phone call from Bill's cell, which was strange since he barely knew how to use it. He only had it because he wanted one. When I answered I heard nothing, but I knew it was him. Still nothing, so I stopped the call and tried to call him back, but to no avail. Finally I called my other two sisters and said I had to go check on Bill and asked if they wanted to go with me. They said yes, so I picked both of them up and we quickly headed to the house. As we pull up we see his truck in driveway, so we know he's home. Right, home but what tragedy waits inside?

We unlocked the door and found him face down on the floor. We couldn't lift him, or turn him over. He was burning up with fever. I walked out on the porch and decided this was serious, and dialed 911.

It didn't take long for the ambulance to arrive. They quickly did their job of assessing the situation, then loaded him up and took him to hospital. He had a urinary tract infection. They said it was mostly due to his dirty condition. I'd known for a long time that he never took showers or baths. I believe it was because he had a fear of falling. Now I am the bad guy.

He goes from hospital to rehab so he can get better with his strength. That did not set well. He wanted to go home. After a two and a half-month stay, he forced me to get him out and take him home.

I did everything I could to get the house ready for his return. I had grab bars installed, I took up the old rugs he could trip on, as well as clean the place up. I was so afraid this will all happen again. He finally comes home and everything seems to be going well for about three weeks. He always drove to the local café for breakfast, but he was too unstable to continue so he quits going for breakfast.

With little choice, I hired nurses to assist with medication, baths, and meals. Of course, Bill wants nothing to do with this. So here I go again. I talk to social workers, they try so hard to help him qualify for assistance. I came over every day to fix him food. All he wants is breakfast. I learned to cook eggs in a microwave, and did pretty well with that. Coffee, toast, keep it soft, and the eggs runny, he has no teeth and, well you get the picture.

He is getting weaker and weaker. The social workers had been so great to me, *Thank you Jesus, you are always there to provide our needs.* They felt like he was really declining. He would not take his medicine properly, not even when it was outlined in pill containers.

I am still there every day and I see that he is

really gone down. One Saturday afternoon in October 2015, after I finished empting trash and cleaning as best I could, *I felt the Holy Spirit say to me, "Today is his day." That is, if he didn't understand and accept Jesus as Savior his eternity would not be settled.* I decided with the Holy Spirit as my guide, to say, "Bill I want to tell you about something that happened to me back in 1969.

I pulled a chair up close so he could hear well. As I began to speak, he became all ears, *(that was You Holy Spirit)*. I started out my conversation: Our first boy Farrell was only 2 years old. As I began: and said, "I was going to church, but was so confused. I just didn't understand why I needed a Savior.

We were all 10 kids raised so strict, and I felt I was ok. But that's not why you are saved. We are all sinners by birth, because of the sin of Adam and Eve. I told him how I got to reading in 1.*John chapter 5, how it says, he that has the son has life, he that does not is condemned in his sin.* That opened my eyes and I accepted Jesus as my Savior.

He begin to say as most unbelievers do, "Those preachers on TV just ask for money and they're phony. "

I began to tell him that not all those on TV are truly believers in Jesus. But when they stand before the Judgment seat of Christ and they say to Jesus. *'But didn't I do this and this in your name, Just like we today may say, didn't I sing in the choir, wasn't I a deacon, and Jesus will say, if they are not believers in the cross of Christ, "depart from me I never knew you,"* (Matthew 7:23*)*.

I told him about all the times he had fallen and someone came by to help him, "That was God Bill, saving you for this day that you could believe and accept Jesus into your heart before it is eternally too late." I wanted to say, "That was God's Grace," but I knew he would not be familiar with God's Grace.

I began to pray. Don't know what I prayed, it was the Holy Spirit, but after I prayed, I turned to him and saw tears streaming down his face, his nose was running, what a sad look of desperation. "Bill if someone came by two to three weeks from now and asks you where you will go when you die, what will you say?" He paused, licked his dry lips, and wiped tears from his eyes.

"To heaven".

I shook my head. "And why would you go to heaven?"

Bill took a long pause and wiped tears from his face. "Because I asked Jesus into my heart."

Hallelujah! Praise the Lord! A sinner has been redeemed. Thank you Jesus, thank you Holy Spirit for being the nudge that day for me to open my mouth and say, just as you Lord had ordained me to do that particular Saturday afternoon in October 2015.

Little did I know that three weeks later he would be in a hospital bed in the home and going speedily downhill? For the last several days on Hospice, he never ate, drank, or opened his eyes.

I was there on November 2, 2015 by his bed when the hospice nurse was in and said he is in the state of dying. He had a very high fever and she called in some meds for him.

She asked if I wanted to go pick them up for her. "I'd rather you go because they may ask a question about something and I would not know the answer." The nurse agreed and left to pick them up. The moment she was gone I stood by Bill's bedside. I had heard that even though a dying person can't respond, they can hear you. So I began to talk to him. I said "Bill, it won't be bad. You'll see momma and daddy, our brother Clyde, our brother Richard, our sister Katy, and it won't be long till we all join you. "

Then I said, "You know Jesus loves you." His one eye barely opened, but I was able to see the blue of his eye and a big tear right in the corner. With his head on his pillow, he moved his eye up and down in a yes signal.

*Oh, Thank you Jesus, my precious Lord. It is just like you to confirm again that he has you and his eternity is secure because of that day three weeks ago when we prayed and Bill asked Jesus into his heart.. Oh, what a Savor, my mighty precious Lord. I will see Bill again when you call me home.*

I begin all the funeral arrangements. I don't think anyone fully understands how much is involved in the preparation when someone passes. That is unless you the reader have gone through it yourselves. I knew he had two burial plots already, so I head to Green Lawn North to make arrangements. His graveside arrangements were set, Paul and Bonnie's Sunday school teacher, who used to be a pastor officiated.

I chose to do a graveside service because Bill

had never been in church to my knowledge, and I knew that they could do wonderful graveside services. I picked the two songs for them to play. *Amazing Grace*, very fitting, and *Jesus Saves, a*lso very fitting. It's November 6<sup>th</sup>, funeral day. Not without hope I go to the graveside service. It was beautiful. Songs from a recorder was played. I had chosen. What a beautiful service.

**Bro. Bill's tombstone/good word**

### *Burial is over Nov. 6th, 2015 – Now the Stress Begins.*

Well, I was somewhat relieved after the funeral. Until I realized all the work that lay ahead. Like any person would, I took a few days to mourn, but I realized how relieved I was to know where Bill was because of his salvation decision back in October, 2015.

First I had to get Bills new Tax ID for the trust. Then I had to wait for the death certificates to be completed since they are a necessity for nearly everything left to handle. His death, and being there in person when he passed, was hard enough, but then to face all the legalities and details of his life left behind would prove overwhelming.

The property is now available for sale, and all the manufacturing equipment needed to be sold. Everything at the house and shop belonged to him, but the property was all in the names of all of us children.

First things first. I decided to hire an auctioneer to sell all the equipment in the 9,000 square foot building. Most of the equipment was old and close to useless, but some was on the newer side. I did not know one machine from another, hence an auctioneer.

I had a revelation on the auction company to use. Thank you Jesus, because that was of God. Back when I would go to a handicap place here in Springfield to get Bill grab bars and helpful equipment, they gave me a pamphlet that had something on it about auctioneers if needed. I really took this as God providing me the right auctioneer.

My brother-in-law is huge fan of going to auctions, one of his favorite pastimes. Of course, he wanted me to use this friend of his. I agreed to meet with him at the shop building. He came and I asked him a few questions, but he didn't even know the names of the equipment, or what its function was, even I knew those answers. The answer to my dilemma was now clear. I was to use the one on the pamphlet that was provided by the handicap place. My revelation had been given. I took many photos which I sent to them, and they said they believed they could do the auction.

It sounds simple and easy to have an auction, but on so much equipment, it is no small matter. It first has to be arranged, organized, and set up. Every single item in that building had to be tagged and categorized for the catalogue they would give to the bidders. The man they sent from the auction company to do this was wonderful. Alone with me and a guy that my brother allowed to stay there at the home place.

My nerves were always on edge. I felt so nervous I thought my life would end, and actually, at that moment, I wanted it to. I got so angry with the man that stayed in the house. He would say, "We should keep that," when the object was junk. I fell over a large amount of stupid old electrical wire and thought I truly broke my arm. But after x-rays, I escaped without any broken bones, just injured tissues, which lasted for a very long time.

You would never believe the mess in that shop building and the house. We had to clean everything out in the house even though it wasn't our intent to sell it at the auction. There were over fifty bags of clothing left by people Bill would allow to stay in the home. It was a five bedroom home and he would allow anyone off the street to stay there. Was he just lonely? Or did they sweet talk him into letting them stay?

I will never fully understand how he was never harmed, but "God was in control," and it just didn't happen. Thank you, Jesus. You had that plan of yours where you knew Bill would be saved at the end of his days on earth. Such a wonderful Savior is Jesus our Lord.

You know out of all the "stuff" that was removed from the house, pictures, small items, I never had any desire to have any of it. It just brought back bad memories of living in the commune.

Well, we move to auction day, February 10, 2015. What a cold, cold day. But not before I had to have the home open house for 2 weekends so people could see what they were buying. Auctions are "As is, where is." Thank God for that because the house had been so run down from lack of care that God knew it would never sell on the Real Estate market.

Again, how precious and all-knowing is my great Lord and savior.

I must insert here how much trouble and how I got scammed by a couple of guys that were hired to get some of the equipment running before the auction. How stupid I was to give them $500.00 up front to work on the equipment that would not start. I even got a signed agreement from them, but think that did any good? No, no, no! So here I go again, trying to find someone that can do this work.

Well, enter my great God again. While at the shop building one day working, getting old paper work thrown away, there is a tap on the door. When I opened the door there was a man there that wore a military veteran's cap. He asked about the platoon boat Bill had sitting outside, and was falling apart. He wondered what I thought it would bring at auction. I said not sure maybe $250.00. He then told me the kind of work he does and I thought, "Bingo!" He was a mechanic by trade and even in his military work. That's all I needed to hear. God had sent him. He was so fair and honest.

He said I could pay him $8.00 hour and he could start right away. Since I desperately needed someone with the knowledge he had, I realized he was the perfect answer. Thank you again my precious Jesus.

As they say, "And the beat goes on." He begin to work on the non-running equipment. The fork lift needed a new starter and the back hoe needed a new clutch. The old antique wench truck was unfixable, but it looked really neat. Ha, ha, ha. I had to laugh or I would continue to cry my way through.

One of the most difficult projects was getting rid of some old concrete trusses that Bill had gotten somehow, but for who knows what? I advertised FREE come and get. Well, no one could pick them up without them crumbling. So guess what? I finally gave up on FREE and said I will pay $1,500.00 for someone to come and take them away.

Turns out there was a wonderful family that needed them to crumble and lay down their long driveway. They were my answer. They brought their own equipment to pick them up and did it all in two days. I was never happier than I was that day to see the bare ground where they had lain for years. My brother Bill was always going to use everything he collected for something. some day.

One bright spot in this chaos; Bill had an old train. He had built track for it and put new seats inside. He also had a caboose on back and a neat engine on the front. A man from Cassville, Mo, wanted that train for the Cassville museum. Turns out that his type of engine and train looked the same as the one that ran through Cassville years ago before they shut down the train station.

I sold the man that train and felt very content. Of course, it wasn't me, it was my God again. I took $8,000, non-refundable deposit, the balance due three days before the Auction. Whew! Things finally had gone better.

After weeks of setting up all the equipment to look as perfect as possible, Auction day finally arrives. Feb 10th had to be the coldest day of the year for sure. Cars were parked everywhere. Thank goodness many were there.

**Last picture of 3 sisters in old Home Place 3005 W. Chestnut Expy. Cold Auction day. Feb. 10, 2016**

Auctioneers began the sale inside with the large equipment, we had a gas heat stove in the office, and that's where the auction people were set up.

That's where I tried to stay as well, but there were countless questions to answer up at the house.

Finally about 1:00 p.m. they said they were going to pause with the inside stuff and auction off the property. My heart drops because earlier a man came up to me and wrote on a piece of paper that there was a man there with him that he thought might be interested. He wrote a figure and asked if it would be enough to buy it. I told him I really wasn't sure because my brother-in-law would have to agree on the price as well. That's the Lt. Coronial again, Bonnie's husband even though I was supposed to be in charge.

This stranger pointed out who the man was and I began to follow him around like a hound dog. I stuck right by him, talking and getting to know him. He had sold a strip of land on his farm to the highway department and had a couple of million dollars from that sale. Is this *the man*? Is this God's plan?

The property auction begins, and I am standing right next to my new best friend at this point. The auctioneer starts the bid out at one million. Nothing happens. He then gets all the way down to $500,000. I nudged my man, "Hey isn't this where you wanted to be?" He immediately raised his hand. There was another man there that wanted the property also. Hum, God's plan. A second bidder, God knows…. My man comes back with the higher bid, the other man takes it, and my man bids higher. The other bidder decided to bow out. The auctioneer thanks him then says, "Sold!" and points to the man next me.

*Lord, I thank you, I thank you!*

We, the family decide the offer is more than acceptable and agree to the sale at the bid price. I immediately take this new friend of mine straight to the office. He has to make a ten-percent deposit and pay the balance at closing. I don't think he knew what hit him, but I do. God had this plan all along.

*Jesus, how kind and loving you are. How without you, we could do nothing. I thank you, I thank you!*

Time to relax on cloud nine thinking that this will all be over soon.

Back into the building to sell the rest of the stuff. Shortly after 4:00 p.m. all that was going to sell has sold. Anything that was too big just couldn't sell. So the man that bought the property got whatever was left. Well, this part of the mess is over. Even though through many toils and snares I had managed to get through, I feared there would still be more to take care of.

Jesus, thank you for all the guidance, and when I cried and prayed, when I thought I would not make it, you were always there to bring me through the fire you brought me through so many times before.

After the final closing sale of the estate it was time to divide the proceeds according to Bill's wishes. Now the fighting among the siblings begins. You didn't think that would go smooth did you? I finally received all the paperwork from the sale, and I collected all the other necessary documents to take to the CPA my husband and I have used for years. Thankfully he was able to advise me how to get my brother's trust wishes completed. I had everything documented and accounted for as I did the first split among the four surviving sisters that Bill named in his trust.

It's not over for about a year, but it is in motion to be completed. Thank you Lord. Each one of the sisters, of course did things a little different.

The sister in Florida bought herself a new car, the youngest sister also bought a new car, my sister with Alzheimer's, of course, was not fully aware of what she had since her husband had power of attorney for her. At this point of my brother Bills death, Bonnie had not died, and that makes it so sad for me, because Bonnie would never know that her share went to her daughter in Washington..

My sister in Florida said, "Bonnie wouldn't have spent it for herself anyway. She's like me. We grew up so poor that I always felt I needed to save every dime I had for a rainy day. I always did just that too, so I did just that--saved it."

Life is strange, we never know how to accept it. We go along, and as a believer we pray, asking God to direct our paths. He does, it's just that we have to follow the crumbles that we can see to know where we are heading.

Now this journey is heading down! As I get back into how this world is going I just know you will have to agree with me.

I'm not happy about it, and I am sad for those reading this that have never taken Jesus, the one that died for your sins, went to that cross, was crucified, bled and died, buried in that borrowed tomb, all for you and me so we could have eternal life.

But, He rose again, resurrected from the dead, ascending to heaven, and as he says in the word, "*I go to prepare a place for you and I will come again to receive you unto myself.*" Hallelujah. Because I have asked Him into my heart, my home is waiting in heaven while we await His return as Revelation tells us.

Will you take a moment right now to understand this? That Jesus was God in the flesh, came as a baby in the manger, went to Calvary, died for your sins and mine, so we could have everlasting life.

Just simply say, "*Jesus I believe you are who you say you are. You came to die for my sins, as we all have sinned and come short of the glory of God.*" (Romans 3:24-25). All have sinned and come short of the glory of God. That's me, that's you. I need you please forgive me of my sins and come into my heart.

Once you truly take Him into your heart, and not just as head knowledge like I told you I had. Until I truly understood how much He loves me and I accepted Him as Savior, then you are saved and have your eternal home in heaven forever and ever, Amen. Go to a Bible believing church, get under the Holy Bible word and grow in grace and knowledge of the mighty Lord, Jesus Christ.

Now that hopefully you are ready for that day of His return. Read Philippians 4:16. *The dead in Christ shall rise first and we that remain shall be caught up to meet them in the sky. And forever we shall be with the Lord.*

## *Bonnie and Alzheimer's*

Before Bills death he had removed my sister Bonnie from being the First Successor Trustee and put me in her place. This was due to her Alzheimer's diagnosis. In the very beginning, along with her husband, I kept saying maybe she just needs some type of medication to help. Maybe she just needs some vitamins that she is short of, Maybe, this maybe that.

I would go with them to her doctor appointments, but that always turned into a family feud. The doctor would say that I am not a family counselor and that Bonnie and her husband needed to work this out. But you see, Bonnie's husband, and their one and only daughter, were the educated. I felt they always made Bonnie feel lower than them, and that hurt her self-esteem. I even felt she was mistreatment, and was put into the same situation, we would all feel the same. Plus it did not help that Bonnie came from life at the Thomas Commune.

Bonnie's husband Paul, is a retired Lt. Colonel, and their daughter Susan, has made a career out of college. She now has a Master's Degree, and I think she will be going for her Doctorate Degree. All of her education happily paid for by daddy. She was and is a daddy's girl.

Although I seem to sound harsh toward her and her dad, I do repent, because I know it has to be very hard being the caregiver of Bonnie that Paul is to her at this point in their lives. I have since learned that her husband has really mourned her situation and I truly repent of my wrong thinking. "Forgive me Lord for seeing things different, and now knowing how good he was to her."

It's been about eight or nine years since Paul first told me of what he felt was going on with Bonnie. Alzheimer's. I refused that word and begin to pray for Bonnie. God has His own plan and it is not getting better. Jesus knows what He has designed for each and every one of His children. Bonnie is one of His children, so I am assured that when she goes, I *will* see her again.

I want to express here how terrible this disease is. I know many of you reading this story have, or has had, a loved one with Alzheimer's. You may have been through this, or are in the process of caring for your loved one now, or have someone in your family with this horrible disease—just know your journey and heartache are shared by many.

I did the walk for Alzheimer's at Jordon Valley Park in Springfield, MO in the summer of 2017. We must find a cure for this terrible disease.

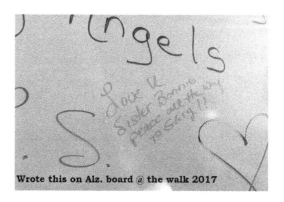

Wrote this on Alz. board @ the walk 2017

Sarah 2018 Walk

It was touching to hear the stories and see the sadness of those that had family members with Alzheimer's, and those that were care givers for them. Also there were many stories from those who lost their loved one to the disease.

This is such a beautiful poem for the Alzheimer's patient:

*Do not ask me to remember,*
*Don't try to make me understand.*
*Let me rest and know you're with me,*
*kiss my cheek and hold my hand.*

*I'm confused beyond your concept.*
*I'm sad and sick and lost.*
*All I know is that I need you.*
*To be with me at all cost.*

*Do not lose your patience with me,*
*do not scold or curse or cry.*
*I can't help the way I'm acting.*
*I can't be different though I try.*

*Just remember that I need you,*
*that the best of me is gone.*
*Please don't fail to stand beside me,*
*Love me till my life is gone.*

**BONNIE SAGERSER 2015**

***We lost Bonnie November 19, 2017.***

Never did I ever believe that she would go that fast. It seems like when she went into the care center two months prior, it was a rapid, downhill slide. My youngest sister, Dixie and I visited her as much as we could bear. It is heartbreaking to see your beloved sister who no longer knows who you are. Yet I had to see her because I loved her, and that part of me said it did not matter if she knew who I was, because I knew who she was.

It is so sad how they go back into their childhood, they talk, as long as they can talk, about the early days in their life because they don't know the current days. They no longer comprehend the current here and now.

We had just seen her after church on November 19, 2017, and she had seemed a little more rousted.

I told Dixie, my youngest sister, we will see her in the morning. I knew she would make it for a few more days. The doctor from Hospice said that she had about 6 days to go.

So after that Sunday afternoon visit, and sure that I would see her Monday morning I headed home. I got phone call from her husband, Paul at 6:10 p.m. He said Bonnie had passed at 6:05.

"Oh no, Paul! I planned to see her in the morning!" God had His plan, and that was the day he planned to take Bonnie home. She knew nothing, and that realization was so very sad to know. But I know she always heard us even if she couldn't respond.

Funeral arrangements were postponed for a week because their daughter, Susan couldn't get plane ticket from Washington State since it was holiday time. So we didn't have the funeral until November 30th. I was allowed to speak at the funeral. I needed to tell everyone I knew just how special Bonnie was.

I went to my computer to compose what I wanted to say, and the words just flowed, all in God's grace, those words were given to me. For Him to get the glory.

So on November 30, 2017, at about 12:15, I stood with my broken heart before the packed funeral home and begin to speak:

### *My Sister Bonnie:*

Bonnie was number five in the line of ten children. With the number five slot you found

Bonnie, who was a built-in mother, sister and friend. But what I want to tell you about her is that she was an example of the Bible reference to Meekness, not weak in strength, but Meekness that shows true strength.

She had true riches, because she had a quiet-meek spirit that revealed what was most important. Never boisterous or bragging, no importance on a big degree, and look at all I have done, but she always put others before herself.

She was very pleased with her husband's accomplishments, making a perfect hostess for his military honors, and she spoke highly of her daughters great intelligence, yet in her quiet meek heart, she had what God would say, "A lady after His own heart," Bonnie knew it was not her, but the Lord that blessed and provided the true meaning to life.

Bonnie was wise and knew that it was not in things and *stuff* we possess, because when the latest gadget breaks, or that heirloom is gone or missing, you realize it is your relationship with your heavenly father that satisfies and endures.

Our love to care for others, does not weather or fad away. Bonnie learned that from a humble upbringing in a poor household of mom, dad, and ten children.

My true last memories of her will stay with me as I mourn her lost.

(1)   Coming over to her home and she would always be putting out bread for the birds. She'd say that God told her to feed his birds. She listened to God, And:

(2)    A couple weeks prior to her becoming bed ridden, I found her setting asleep in the care center recreation room area, after patting her leg and trying to wake her, I said, "Bonnie let's get up and walk the hall some." I took her hands and pulled her up. When she stood in front of me I put my arms around her, and she put her arms around me. We just stood there for the longest time just hugging—sister to sister.

I said, "Bonnie, I love you," she said, as well as she could, "I lov…you too……

So when we meet again in our heavenly home, I will hug her and say, "I came as soon as God would let me so we could say I love you again. Where Bonnie is, you could not get her to come back. No, no, no. Heaven is worth it all.

Are you ready for that *Call Home*? Do you know Jesus as your sin forgiver? Who so ever calls on the name of the Lord shall be saved (Romans 10:13). Bonnie really wants you to know that. Especially after she is there and seen, *not* just heard, "How beautiful heaven must be."

This is a little Bible tract from a former pastor I loved:

A person may go to heaven:
    (1)    Without wealth
    (2)    Without beauty
    (3)    Without learning
    (4)    Without fame
    (5)     Without culture
    (6)    Without friends

## BUT NO ONE CAN GO TO HEAVEN WITHOUT CHRIST.

For there is no other name under heaven given among men, whereby we must be saved (Acts 4:12).

As I remember all these hardship times, I remember...

Bonnie went from driving, doing all the things she wanted to do, going with her sisters to visit our brother, to finally having her car taken from her. That move took away her freedom. I fought this on her behalf until Paul had to tell me she had gotten lost, not once, but several times. I then knew that it was dangerous for her and to succumb to his decision on her behalf.

Paul had Alzheimer's on his side of his family so I know he knew what was coming. It was more difficult for us since we never had such experience on our side. When Bonnie was put into the Alzheimer's care center, I think she just decided to succome to her destiny. She barley lasted a month. It is almost funny to me now how she would go from room to room at night, she wouldn't sleep. She would take little things from the rooms, but of course other patients did the same thing. That's just the way of the Alzheimer patient.

Bonnie, seemed like she became mad, hurt, and reverting back into the home commune dysfunctional family that she remembered. I do not know what she knew, or did not know, but she took it all out in what she knew were her last days. It's like she was never the person she was meant to be by our heavenly Father, and she gave up on her dreams and decided to be aggressive in those final days. In her normal state, before the Alzheimer's, she was a believer in Jesus and was very active in the church, helping in every way she could, that was a beautiful thing because she had Jesus as her Savior. The scripture says, "*There is no condemnation to those in Christ Jesus*," (Romans 8:1).

God saw, God knew Bonnie was His child even though her brain changed. Hallelujah, thank you Jesus for your marvelous Grace.

Life is such a struggle. I have never seen it as bad as it seems to be now. The only thing I do know, is that God does allow things into our life for a reason. Nothing, even if it comes from Satan first, has to pass through the permission of our God.

## CHAPTER ELEVEN

### *The World is a Changin'*

Hang on it's going to show you how things is a Fallen' very fast.

Headlines of this world as we read them each day:

More and more terror attacks around the world.

More and more churches now have gun patrolmen in their houses of worship.

Did you ever think, that in the United States of America, it could be un-safe safe to go to the house of God? As you have been reading over and over in the news and on TV, churches are becoming a target for shootings. Vigils are held for the victims of these tragedies.

The most disaster money ever was spent last year. To date, the total for 2017 is over six-billion dollars.

Riots and protesting is everywhere.

Listen to these statistics and from not so very long ago... I am nearly 75 and the following things were not on the scene.

I do Remember TV as I was about twelve. But it was snowy screen and hard to make out pictures.

So here we go before I was a youngster there was:

- No televisión
- No penicillin
- No polio shots
- No frozen foods
- No Xerox
- No contact lenses
- No Frisbees and
- No birth control pill
- No credit cards
- Laser beams
- Ball point pens
- Panty hose
- Air conditioners
- Dishwashers
- Clothes Dryers
- Space travel (only in Flash Gordon books)

## *In My Day*

- Every family had a father and a mother
- The woman and the man were married before they lived together
- We always called a woman older than us "mam"
- All men were called "sir", including policemen
- There were no Gay Rights, computer-dating. dual careers, daycare centers
- No group therapy
- Our lives were governed by the Bible, good judgment, and common sense.
- We were taught the difference between right and wrong, and to take responsibility for our actions.
- Serving our country was a privilege
- Living in this country was a bigger privilege.
- Draft dodgers were scorned
- Time-sharing meant time the family spent together in the evenings and weekends
- NO FM radio, tape decks, electric typewriters, yogurt, or guys wearing earrings
- We listened to Big Bands, Jack Benny, and the President's speeches on our radio. (No kid blew his brains out listening to Tommy Dorsey.)
- Anything stamped with "Made In Japan" on it was considered junk

- The term making out, referred to how you did on your school exam
- Pizza Hut, McDonald's, and instant coffee were not around
- We had five and dime stores where you could actually buy things for five and ten cents
- Ice Cream cones, phone calls, Pepsi and rides on a streetcar were all a nickel.
- You could spend your nickel on enough stamps to mail a letter or two postcards.
- You could buy a new Ford Coupe for $ 600.00 (Still hard to afford)
- Gasoline was eleven cents a gallon.
- Grass was mowed.
- Coke was a cold drink
- Pot was something your mother cooked in
- Rock music was your grandmother's lullaby
- Aids were helpers in the school principal's office
- Chip meant a piece of wood
- Hardware was found in the hardware store
- Software was not even a word
- We were the last generation to believe a lady needed a husband to have a baby
- It is sad to say good-by to some of these things. It makes you realize how far the *decay and the downfall* of AMERICA has come, and this is all since the 50"s. This spurs the thought, "How low can we go?"

I will continue to where we are today, 2018 and the disasters that are all around us.

SARAH TYLER

*Headlines Across the News Show Decline:*

- California floods and mud slides
- School shootings at an all time high
- Teens dropping rocks off of overpasses onto cars below
- Trucks used to plow into crowds to kill as many people as possible
- Terror attacks hit an all time high
- Schools no longer allow prayer anywhere on their grounds
- Atheist groups are allowed to have after school meetings on school grounds
- Colleges will not allow conservative speakers on campus
- One movie star brandished a bloody, decapitated head of President Trump
- A popular singer in a protest crowed loudly screamed, "I have often     thought about blowing up the White House with no action taken against her.
- No legal action was taken against either of the women who disrespected the President of the United States. Whether or not they like who is President, they have the responsibility to respect the office he holds. In my opinion, I think they should have both been arrested on the spot and put in jail

Christians are being prosecuted all over the world. Some foreign countries arrest them, torture them, and refuse to release them. I could go on and on, but I am sure you understand what I'm saying about our world today.

These are the signs of the times the Bible speaks of in the end times. Please watch your headlines in the newspapers. Listen to what you hear on television and oh, just in case some of you still listen to radio, it's on there as well.

### SIGNS OF THE LAST DAYS:

(1)  Lover of self
(2)  Love death
(3)  Loving things (Luke 12-13-15)
(4)  Poison of pornography
(5)  Greed of gambling
(6)  Monster beverage (alcohol 7)

What can you do to save America? When we are so split? Lord have mercy.

One of the greatest divides I have ever witnessed is one ethnic group against another ethnic group. I thought that was all over. The Bible speaks of this great divide (Matthew 24:7).

Well, not in this fallen world that we find ourselves in.

### *More and More Protests Are Happening:*

Not only in America, but all around the world, people protest about, "Black lives matter!" They do. But all lives matter. That seems to be a fact that the protesters forget in their rush to make their point to the crowd, the world, or whoever is listening to them.

Now we see that terrorists have come across our borders, and they use new and old methods to kill as many people as they can. Their main weapon of choice is a large vehicle and they drive it into the largest crowd they can find at the time. Not just in America, but all over the world. Whether you like or dislike President Trump, you must admit; he has been put under the magnifying glass like no other president in history. Is this just a sign of the times? Because I do believe he was prayed into office by Christian believers. We had to have this change for America.

Don't you long for the "Old America"? Mom, apple pie and Baseball? How did we ever get to this terrible decline of morals and decay? Television shows have become bad examples of family life for our youth, and theaters are running more and more

R-rated movies that have become immoral.

People have turned to Netflix's for their movie watching since the choices are nearly unlimited. There are some children's movies, but the adults watch some of the worst. It's just a bad, bad, world we are living in. A Fallen world as my title says.

The Christian prosecution is on the rise. Look at what you see happening to those that are believers in our Lord Jesus Christ. I am seeing all this unfold before my eyes and I am so troubled in what is to come for the unbeliever.

I know it may be hard for you as you read, and maybe you have never trusted in Jesus as your sin forgiver, but all these things I am writing about are events in my own life that I have witnessed personally, and some of the things I should have done differently.

I write this to help warn you that I have been through all this, and I know that many of you have been through even worse situations. I have known family turmoil, physical and mental abuse, along with health issues like cancer, Alzheimer's, heart attacks, drug and alcohol abuse. I have had to go to court to help family members. I had to have one younger sister put in a nursing home to dry out Thank God that turned to be a good thing. She was cured and remains dry and sober now, twelve years later. Praise God!

As we continue on with this personal writing I want to help you understand how to overcome dangers, toils and snares that can be avoided in your life.

(1) We have an advocate with our heavenly Father.

(2) When God saw that man needed to be redeemed he knew he must come in the form of a man to live and feel as the man he had created.

(3) I know you may not feel like it at times, but as we hurt, cry, and feel pain, so does our God, because he took on flesh and feels what we feel.

(4) He never intended for us, His creations, to have to suffer the pain (which is sin), but because He created us with a free choice, we sometimes make bad choices.

(5) You, like me, have had times where you couldn't understand why little children had to suffer. My friends, SIN is the reason. Not their fresh little hearts of sins, because the babies and little children don't know about sin. But remember, all have sinned and come short of the glory of God. The amazing thing about little children when they die and are not old enough to understand there is a Savior, God promises He will take them to himself.

(6) You, like me, have probably watched our world go from loving one another to hating one another. Another sign of last days.

(7) Unloving attitudes haunt our world. I have never seen such hatred against certain races, against our police force, our military, and against our currently elected President of the United States. This President has been crucified more than any other American President in history.

(8) Yes, there is certainly a change in our world.

(9) Do you see that we as Christians are under

attack like never before?

(10) This is all in the Bible as coming to pass in the last days.

So how do we know how to walk in *such a time as this?* There is only one way and that is to stay focused on God. *He will never leave you or forsake you* (Hebrews 13:5).

I personally feel an attack by Satan when I hit like on Facebook in an effort to encourage people in their times of need. You could spend hours just praying for each prayer request you read on Facebook.

There are so many people with desperate needs. Sickness, children problems, financial problems, the list goes on and on. You the reader have your own list of needs. But I have found that each and every time I go through a crisis, I come through it with a stronger will to live for God. I believe this is where He wants us to be.

Remember we are Heaven bound and this world is just a temporary home. We are *being* prepared for that much better place. Take a moment to reflect on all you have been through up until this time. Think carefully about all the years that have gone by. I think, if you are a believer in our Lord Jesus Christ, then you can see that what I am saying is true. I only wish I had found Jesus sooner. There are so many that need Him and I, knowing that he is *"The Way the truth, and the life,"* (John 14; 16). I should have told so many more.

Why do you think we are so afraid to just simply tell the "Good News? We have it when we know Jesus, but we let Satan, the great deceiver, the great liar, convince us that we will be thought of as weird.

As I have been through things just like you, I have found that we must take our stand. Jesus will give us, has given us, His Holy Spirit to guide and lead to open our mouths. You must be in His word, the Bible daily to be able to fight the fiery darts of the Devil. I have found in my Christian walk, that if we just tell how we found him, our testimony, that God will use that to bring a lost sinner to Himself.

If you have named Christ as your only God and Savior, you have declared independence from the rule of sin and Satan over your life. You have been set free. As Colossians 1:13 tells us, *"For He rescued us from the domain of darkness, and transferred us to the Kingdom of His beloved Son."* Having declared spiritual independence from the rule of Satan, though, you may be wondering why then are you still in a fight?.

When you ask and are curious about why it often feels like you are still in a battle. Just like America didn't secure her freedom simply by asking or declaring it to be so, Satan is not about to let you go without putting up his opposition. Satan knows if he lets you out from under his influence, you become too dangerous to his agenda. Instead of him telling you what to do, you will be telling him what you are going to do.

That doesn't set well with Satan at all. Even though you have been legally set free from the reign of sin in your life, Satan does not want you to expediently set free. My hope for you dear friends, is that you will be brought into the full realization, and experience *your* spiritual freedom. May you see this to be truth and cling to that blessed hope that, "He that is free is Free Indeed?"

## CHAPTER TWELVE

### *Preparing You for Eternity*

The battle on the Christian road

I know now I have believed. I have no doubt of that Jesus, God's son. God in the flesh is truly *my Savior*. I know that He is the Way the Truth and the Life.

Let's look at the power and the miracles that God has done throughout our lives. I have learned that in praying, that it is when you deeply *believe* that God really listens to my prayers.

When we are desperate, and our lives are in turmoil, that's when we see His mighty works. Follow along in the Bible at the miracles God performed through the son and the Holy Spirit. Abraham and Sara: God gave them the promised child at his age of 100 and Sara at 90. Now that's a miracle.

When God called Moses to free his people, take them out of Egypt, Moses rebelled and gave excuses, but God never leaves His plan undone. He led Moses to do as He wanted him to do. Moses performed miracles, such as parting the Red Sea to save his people from the Romans who pursued them. God provided food, shelter, and even though it was fallen from the sky, bread, (Manna) when the Israelites complained, That God provide then with quail, meat.

When we look at Psalms 104-1-8, we really see *How great thou art My heavenly father*. You have created all things and all for your good pleasure.

I look at all I have been through, and all I took for granted until I was on the path of the Christian road. Even though there are many hardships and many mistakes made in my life after becoming a Christian, I know now that He is leading me. God is leading me wherever that destiny takes me. I am at a real cross road in my life now.

Never did I think I would not know what career I was to follow. I still don't know what happened to that girl inside of me that gave me confidence, never being uncertain in making the right decisions in my life. I believe it is Satan trying to take away the joy of my salvation.

I love to be certain that people know the Lord Jesus as their Savior before it is eternally too late, and because I love to see people reach the greatest potential God has given them, Satan doesn't like that. But even when I show people all they can be, it causes conflict in our relationship. They take it as meddling in their life. I suppose you could call it meddling, but I assure you it is with good intentions that I offer my advice.

Our world has turned from the love chapter of

the Bible (1.Corinthians 13) to people just tossing away unneeded things in their lives. They have turned the love chapter of the Bible from the Love of the Bible to the love of the world.

It's now popular to flip-flop the qualities described in this chapter reversing and refining love. The world, which obsesses about love, has made biblical love unpopular, scorned, and belittled. What the Bible in the love chapter shows us is now completely turned upside down. *Love does not envy, yet the world is motivated by envy* (1.Corinthians 4).

The scriptures tell us to love one another, but the fallen world has reversed that to love ourselves above all others. We are a generation of miss-hap people. People that say we are one thing, but our fruits and actions show much different. Will it take the coming of the Lord to put all things in order? I believe that it will.

Are you ready, like I am, to look at the world prophecies and see just where we are in this stage of life events? Are you ready to see just how close His return is?

### *God's Purpose and Plan*

Well, now I will begin to tell you how I see this world doing its great fall. It has been doing this from the 50's onto the time we are living in now.

To explain how I see this world continually falling, I will give you just what morals and decline is as stated. We see the decline of life as I knew it. Articles will follow as I show you just how low can we go? When you scratch your head and say, "Where as parents, raising our children, did we go wrong? Didn't we provide everything they needed?" All but love and care as God directs in His Word!

Some of the signs of this great falling process will follow as I give you statistics on how we started and where we are even at this point.

A little--very little progress is being made by researchers on AIDS. AIDS spreads from the homosexual community to the heterosexual community. It's ironic, that the old fashioned virtue of sex with a permanent partner, the Biblical standard of the past, is now regarded as the number one principal protection against the scourge. To be moral, to be monogamous, is now the greatest defense against the new plague

In many ways, the 1950s were better than the 1980s, because the highest Moral code ever given to man was followed by a majority of the people. That did not make it right, but it was followed, it made a better world in which to live. Let us ever follow that moral, code given by God - by so doing we will have the best life here on earth and prepare ourselves for that world to come in which nothing immoral will exist.

Other signs of the Fallen World: Atheists (non-believers of our creator God) are very bold now. They have become a movement and even have their own groups. They meet, and because it seems like all need a GOD, the atheists have theirs. They want to worship Satan. It is even proclaimed that our schools are to allow an after school club for Satan worshipers.

Even the (Christian) born again believers don't know their Bible's, so they don't see where they are at this given time in scripture. I personally believe, and you may disagree, but when our borders were left open, with not one to stop the illegals from entering our country, that along with those illegals, they brought in their gods. This was the biggest start to the decline of our Christian nation. Remember, God said in His Holy word, "*I will have no other gods before me.*" (Exodus 20:2)

Jesus is profaned, no respect for the church or for worship. At this point I must include that all the movements that have started in the last decade are from the lack of "authority, and respect." I can see where this lies in the upbringing of children by their parents.

And this is where we see the domino effect. Bad parents breed bad kids, bad kids grow up and have children, (mainly out of wed lock) and the beat goes on, and the beat goes on.

Now man can marry man, and woman can marry woman. And to make it even worse, these couples can adopt children. Oh, My Lord, how confused this must make that child. No wonder we have so much chaos in this old fallen world. I feel so bad for the little children that are put into this setting. They will grow up confused.

God intended for a man and a woman to have the children. Why can't humans understand that? Even the animal kingdom doesn't do that. It takes a male and female to produce an off spring. Sorry, you just can't get a child into a female's womb without that male sperm. Shouldn't that tell us something? But no, the human race continues to decline.

*Oh, Lord Give us help from trouble, for vain is the help of man. Through God we shall do valiantly; for He it is that shall tread down our enemies* (Psalms108: 12-13).

When will we learn that with God all things are possible?

It is still so alarming to walk through this world as it is now, "A fallen world" I so await with anticipation in which nothing immoral will exist. We are told of all this in the scriptures. Read the account in Matthew chapter 24 of the Holy Bible. Marriage is defined from a law passed Feb. 23, 2011 from the United States Government Attorney General and Congress, the law is called in defense of marriage: DOMA. Both houses of congress passed the bill and it was signed into law by President Clinton in 1996.

In 1977 fewer than one million Americans were living as sex couples, living together unmarried. In 2007 that rose to 6.4 million. See the decline? Humans were created as both physical and spiritual beings. So as the physical being goes in an unspiritual direction so goes the morality.

### *Remember when these codes were in effect?*
- Be honest
- Live a chaste life
- Obey the laws of the land, (what happened to that?) What happened to the Constitution?
- Use clean language
- Respect others.

• Abstain from alcoholic beverages, substance abuse.

• Participate regularly in church services

• Observe the dress and grooming standards

• Encourage others in their commitment to comply with any Honor Code

Let's Take A Look

Closer and closer, we will see: Prophecy in the making.

Jesus is coming again. It's in your Bible. "*In My father's house are many mansions; if it were not so, I would have told you. I go to prepare a place for you. And if I go and prepare a place for you, I will come again and receive you to myself; that where I am, there you may be also,*" (John 14:2-3).

There are signs of Jesus' second coming. It's in the Bible. "*Then He spoke to them in a parable: Look at the fig tree, and all of the trees. When they are already budding, you see and know for yourselves that summer is now near. So you also, when you see these things happening, know that the Kingdom of God is near,*" (Matthew 24:29-31).

What are some of these signs?. "As Jesus was sitting on the Mount of Olives, the disciples came to him privately. " *Tell us,*" they said, "*when will this happen, and what will be the sign of your coming and the end of the age?*" (Matt 24; 3.)

Men posing as Jesus will try to deceive people in the last days. "*At that time if anyone says to you, "look here is the Christ", or There He is! Do not believe it, for false Christ's and false prophets will appear and perform great signs and miracles (to deceive even the elect Christians) if that were possible.*" (Matthew 24; 23-24.)

### Second Coming Signs

There will be wars. Though they may seem overwhelming, it is not the end. It's in the Bible, , You will hear of wars and rumors of wars, but see to it that you are not alarmed. Such things must happen, but the end is still to come." (Matthew 24:6.)

The Second Coming does not come until *after* the Rapture.

## RAPTURE OF THE BELIEVERS.

Non- Christians will find it hard to believe we are living in the last days of earth's history.

"*First I want to remind you that in the last days*

*there will be scoffers who will do all wrong they can think of. And laugh at the truth. This will be their line of arugment: So Jesus promised to come back, did he? Then where is He? He'll never come! Why, as far back as anyone can remember everything has remained exactly as it was since the day of creation.*" (11 Peter 3; 3-4.)

The coming of the Antichrist is a sign of the end. "Little children, it is the last hour: and as you have heard that the Antichrist is coming, even now many is coming, even now many Antichrists have come, by which we know that it is the last hour." (1 John 2; 18.) I may add at this point also that there are many false preachers on the airways. It is sad that they are teaching false doctrines. Many are greedy and always trying to get you to send money, saying this will send blessings to you. God will deal with that as they stand before the Great White Throne of judgment.

As they say, "But didn't we cast out demons? Didn't we serve as deacons in the church, didn't we sing in the church choir? On and on. But our heavenly father knows the heart. He knows if you did the service in the name of Jesus and for His glory or for your own greed and glory. He will say in that day, "Depart from me I never knew you." (Matthew 7; 21-23.)

How truly sad that will be. I have been in church and under the word for nearly fifty-three years now. And I have seen sin abound in my life as well as what I saw in those around me. But the one great thing is; you have Jesus as your Savior, you truly have trusted Him, and then your sins are forgiven.

Past, present and future sins. Sounds too good to be true, but that is what the

Bible says. That's why God came in the flesh to take the penalty for all our sins. When he died on that cross and shed his righteous blood, that was our HOPE for seeing heaven. He was our sacrifice for the sins we are have committed.

The difference with that and the false teachers, and with God saying, "Depart from me I never knew you," is simply, that the one he says that to, really never took Jesus as savior, just used the name of Jesus for their own gain.


### *To Follow-up on Living in the Last Days*

What moral conditions will be characteristic of society in the last days? Mark this: "*There will be terrible times in the last days. People will be lovers of themselves, lovers of money, boastful, proud, abusive, disobedient to their parents, ungrateful, unholy, without love, unforgiving, slanderous, without self-control, brutal, not lovers of good, rash. Conceited, lovers of pleasure rather than lovers of God- having a form of godliness but denying its power. Have nothing to do with them.*" (II Timothy 3:1-5,)

What other signs of the last days does the Bible mention? "There will be signs in the sun, moon and stars. On the earth. Nations will be in anguish and perplexity at the roaring and tossing of the sea. Men will faint from terror, apprehensive of what is coming on the world, for the heavenly bodies will be shaken." (NIV Luke 21; 26-26.)

Talk of peace and safety are a sign of the last days., NIV. "For you know very well that the day of the Lord will come like a thief in the night, while people are saying, "Peace and safety. Destruction will come on them suddenly, as labor pains on a pregnant women, and they will not escape," (I Thessalonians 5; 2-3.)

The gospel will go to all the whole world and the end will come. "*So be prepared, for you don't know what day your Lord is coming. Just as man can prevent trouble from thieves by keeping watch for them, so you can avoid trouble by always being ready for my unannounced return.*" (Matthew 24: 42-44.)

"*Now when these things begin to happen, look up and lift up your heads, because your redemption draws near.*" (Luke 21: 28.)

But remember, this all will be taking place in what Revelation says is the Great seven years of Tribulation. The Rapture of the believers will have happen prior to the start of this great signs. Even though we as believers do see a lot of these signs taking place, thank God we will miss the Tribulation period and we will be coming back with Jesus at the Second Coming. (I Thessalonians 4: 6-17.) Thankfully there will be "*Tribulation saints that are saved during that Tribulation period*" (Revelation 11: 1-13.)

I'm asking again. Are you ready for that Rapture Day and are you coming back with Jesus on the Second Coming?

## CHAPTER THIRTEEN

## *What I've Learned in My Christian Journey*

This has been my Christian Journey through a Fallen World. A life that I can tell you was *hard*. I know Jesus never promised "a rose Garden", but I do know what He did mean when *He created this world and all its splendor, to make it perfect.*.(John 10:10.)

But because of the sin that entered from Adam and Eve it didn't get to be as he wanted. He created man with a free will choice.

Lord put a guard over my mouth. No matter how good I think my intentions are to help, please let nothing come out of my mouth that is not from you.

May you Oh Lord take complete control of my words, my deeds, my thoughts and keep me always obeying you and your word. Direct my path, take me to where you want my life to go as I enter my final days. Oh, how I look forward to seeing you my great Savior, face to face.

While I traveled this journey in this book, I found out things about myself like:

- I found God's gifts in me. Knowing whose I am, helps me express who I am.
- I found my strengths, as I went through the hardships I never thought I could do, and looking back, really don't know how I did go through them.
- I found my weaknesses. I am very emotional and cry so easy. I don't take criticism easily, I have many doubts in my decisions, and I become discouraged in life.
- I found my personality traits: I am a friendly person, I have a caring heart, and I am warm to people wanting to help at a cost to me many times.

In my journey I did make a few wrong decisions--like going into Real Estate. Was this of God? Or was it because my youngest sister came to live with us and said she would pay my way if I would start Real Estate school with her. Did I pray about this? No. I just took for granted that I should do it. I passed the Real Estate Agent test and she didn't.

What did that mean? I worked at real estate and it seemed to be a good field for me. I even went on in 2000 to try for my broker's exam. I did get that, after third try. But was that a good thing? I really enjoy seeing someone made happy

I also have learned there are consequences to the choices we make.

I have found that the Christian path is a struggle and challenging road.

I have found that your prayer life is "the life" God gives us with so many promises, and I can say that He has been faithful in those promises to me through my journey.

I really learned that as we pray, we are to have the faith God instills to us. But without Him you cannot have the faith. And without you, He will not act on your faith.

We must ask in prayer for Him to give us that strong faith to believe. "Believing is seeing".

I've learned that bad things do happen to good people, but we never go through a fiery trial without it making us stronger.

I've learned that you can raise your children the very best way you know, but you must turn them loose as they marry and have their own life. As much as you want to help them, which I so wanted to do, you can't change them except through prayer. God can do anything.

I have really learned that *we all need Jesus*. Best decision I ever made in my journey.

*If we confess our sins, he is faithful and just to forgive us our sins and purify us from all unrighteousness.* (I John 1-9.)

And as John 3:-16 says, "*For God so loved the world that he gave his only begotten son, and whosoever believe in him, shall not perish but have everlasting life.*"

As I age I find so many things that meant so much and were so important to me, are not so important anymore. Is this God's way to show us, "*That this is not our real home, we are only passing through?*" (I Peter 2:11.)

"So teach us to number our days, that we may apply our hearts unto wisdom. "Teach us that is" to reflect on the brevity of life." (NLV. Psalms 90:12.)

If you are reading this true story of one lady's account of her personal life as she walks "My Christian journey through a fallen World," then you may see things different from me. But one thing is absolute in this story: We are all only walking through this journey as a human person, and we all have many different detours in our lives. No matter how you feel about life, and what and why you have gone through your trials and struggles, it was planned and had a purpose by our mighty God.

I would like to leave you in this chapter with all these scriptures that are promises from God in the Bible. Please take time to look them up. There are so many, and when you start to doubt that there is a loving God, turn to some of these scriptures and reflect on how much He has promised us.

Your first step of course is to make sure that you have trusted Jesus, God's son, God in the flesh as your own personal savior. "*For all have sinned and come short of the glory of God*". (Romans 3:23.) And the Romans guide to your salvation (10-9-10).

If you declare with your mouth Jesus is lord, and believe in your heart that God raised him from the dead, you will be saved. "For it is with your heart that you believe and are justified, ("just as if you never sinned ") and it is with your mouth that you profess your faith and are saved. (NIV.)

Ask Jesus into your heart, that's what my brother did three weeks before God took him home, (in my story) and that's what my sister Katy did before her suicide in this story.

*There is no condemnation to those in Christ Jesus. You are saved.* ( 8:1.) Now for the promises that I hold dear as I continue my Christian journey through a fallen world.

Exodus 14:-14 the Lord will fight for you, you need only to be still.

Isaiah 40:-29. He gives strength to the weary, and increases the power of the weak.

Isaiah 40:-31

Psalms 90 (What a promise. I prayed this for my son during his entire tour in Iraq.)

Isaiah 41:-10

Isaiah 41:-13

Isaiah 43:-2, 54: 17, 61:1

More promises: Take time to look these up and read. Claim these words for your own journey.

James 1:5
I John 4:7
II Chronicles 7:14
Deuteronomy 31:8
Jeremiah 29:11
John 3:16
John 3:36
John 8:36
Malachi 3:10
Mark 11:24
Philippians 1:9
Psalms 34:17

*Be anxious for nothing, but in everything by prayer and supplication, with thanksgiving, let your requests be made known to God and the peace of God which surpasses all, understanding will guard your hearts and minds through Christ Jesus.* (Philippians 4:6-7.)

I must admit, this is one that has been my biggest struggle though my walk. And I know that to not trust God and his perfect plan is a sin. So I continue to work daily on this promise. What is your biggest struggle? What do you need help with? I want to assist you to find what I found as I walked through this fallen world. You know that is why we have the struggles, the trials, the worries, because we are in a fallen world.

As I have tried to explain in this story, that because we are getting closer and closer to the "end time", our walk gets harder and harder. We should not be surprised at the things that are happening everyday when we turn on our news television station, or read in the headlines of our local newspaper.

It is going to happen as the scripture tells us, so let's pull together and stay close to the word of God, our solace in this dreaded times. He died for us to give us life. Look up your redemption draws near and nearer.

I went to a missionary's funeral. His name was Charles, and he and his wife were Missionaries' in Pakistan for 59 years. His wife passed three years back, and now it was his time to be called home, to his Heavenly Home. This was something he had written in the obituary pamphlet that I thought was so fitting, I wanted to leave this thought with you. I know Charles, , a great soul winner from mission work in Pakistan, would want you to know these words.

So by permission:

## I SEE THE BEAUTIFUL POEM

I see the meaning of the cross,
That awful, blood-stained, Roman tree,
Christ brought me back from certain death.
By dying on there he set me free.
I see the meaning of the tomb,
That open, empty, borrowed grave,
It could not hold the son of God.
Nor can it whom He would save.
I see the meaning of the cup and the leavened,
broken bread.
As sure as He has died for me I do not look at
death with dread.
I see the meaning of His call,
"Come thou and follow me"
No more I live as I would choose,
Lord, let me live my life for Thee.
By Charles E. Coleman, Retired Missionary

When the saved in Jesus Christ die, there is rejoicing in heaven. No more tears, no more pain. We are whole again, praise God. Because we have finally come home to our great and loving creator.

My husband and I have a saying: When he leaves for work or I am leaving our home, we say, "See you at the House."

That's our house, "The House" in heaven.

I pray that this is your House also.

See You At The House!

Blessing and glory and honor unto the King.

## CHAPTER FOURTEEN

### *Waiting His Soon Return*

I am meditating, being very relaxed while I write these final words, knowing that I really have no control on what will be the next events to take place. It's just that all I have told you in the journey are not just words, but signs and wonders that are leading to the final *Big* event.

I understand that as you read the account of "my journey", and knowing you have yours also, that you have seen that all of this was leading somewhere.

That somewhere is *God's Soon Return*.

All the signs are in place. Prophecy that was foretold many, many years ago that has led us to the signs of the times today. It's not something to dread, but something to look forward to.

How sometimes I just set and think about my loved ones, who I truly knew had Jesus as their Savior, how much I wish I could be there with them also.

If you knew what I even know from my times of

scripture reading, of Bible teaching, from pastor preaching, you would understand why it's a *good thing*, not a bad thing.

How amazing it must have been for the Apostle John as it is foretold in Revelations Four. John sees a door opened in heaven and he hears the sound of a trumpet telling him to "*come up hither*" John, as a member of the faithful Church, is taken up in the spirit to see the things in heaven. I believe the apostle Paul also saw some of those things when he was caught up too.

*After this I looked, and a door was opened in heaven; and the first voice which I heard was as if it were a trumpet talking with me; which said,. "Come up hither, and I will show thee things which must be hereafter."* John sees a door opened in heaven and he hears the sound of a trumpet telling him to "*come up hither* "

The spirit indwelt Church will hear these same words at the rapture.

John, is taken up in the spirit to see the things in heaven.

*And immediately I was in the spirit; and behold, a throne was set in heaven, and one sat on the throne. And he that sat was to look upon like a jasper and a stone; and there was a rainbow round about the throne, in sight like unto an emerald,*

*John was in his body and was taken immediately up to the third heaven.*

*He said he did not know if he went in his body or departed from his physical body. Paul could write also about the mystery of the rapture of the Church in his letters because he also had a foretaste of it when he was caught up to the third heaven.*

*Paul confirms this also: As he says in II Corinthians 12: 2. I knew a man in Christ about fourteen years ago, whether in the body, I cannot tell; God knoweth; such as one Caught up to the third heaven. Then John continues as he says in Revelation. John tells us about the throne he saw in heaven and the description of the one who sat on the throne.* (The text in this passage should say and there sat on the throne, not one sat on the throne. The word *one* is not in the Greek text.)

John and the church are in the spirit looking upon the throne of God. the Father was certainly there with Jesus on his throne but since scripture tells us that no man, except the Son, and that no man could see the Father and live. John could only have seen the son of God

*As john 1:18 says, "'No man hath seen God at any time; the only begotten Son, which is in the bosom of the Father, he hath declared him."* What is actually seen here by John is Jesus sitting on the Father's throne. Jesus is the image of the Father.

*Who being the brightness of his glory, and the express image of his person, and upholding all things by the word of his power, when he had by himself purged our sins, sat down on the right hand of the Majesty on high.* (Hebrews 1:3.)

The description that John gives also indicates that he sees Jesus. *The high priest; the jasper and sardine are the first and last stones in the breastplate of the high priest* (Exodus 28; 17-21).

*The son of God from eternity past to the eternity future, is reigning upon the throne of the Father.*

*The rainbow around the throne is a refraction of the full spectrum of light coming from God, the emerald is the stone of the tribe of Judah, the rainbow that had the appearance of an emerald did so because the light was shining through Jesus who came from the tribe of Judah.*

*And around about the throne were four and twenty seats; and upon the seats I saw four and twenty elders sitting in white rainment; and had on their heads crowns of gold.*

*Scripture says the Twelve Apostles of the inner circle of Jesus will rule over the twelve tribes of Israel, but these twenty-four surround the throne of father God, and apparently rule over all creation.*

*The four and twenty elders fall down before him that set on the throne, and worship him that liveth forever and ever and ever, and cast their crowns before the throne, saying, "Thou art worthy, O lord, to receive glory and honor and power: for thou hast created all things, and for thy pleasure they are and were created."*

### The Revelation Continues

*And I saw in the right hand of him that sat on the throne, a book written within and on the backside, sealed with seven seals. And I saw a strong angel proclaiming with loud voice, who is worthy to open the book, and loose the seals thereof?*

*And no man in heaven, nor on earth, neither under the earth, was able to open the book, neither to look thereon.*

*And I wept much, because no man was found*

*worthy to open and to read the book, neither to look thereon. And one of the elders saith unto me, weep not;*

*Behold, the lion of the tribe of Judah, the Root of David, hath prevailed to open the book, and to loose the seven seals thereof.*

*And I beheld, and lo, in the midst of the throne and of the four beasts, and in the mist of the elders, stood a Lamb as it had been slain, having seven horns and seven eyes, which the seven Spirits of God are sent forth into all the earth.*

*And he came and took the book out of the right hand of him that sat upon the throne.*

*And when he had taken the book, the four beasts and twenty elders fell down before the Lamb, having every one of them harps, and golden vials full of odors, which are the prayers of saints. And they sung a new song, saying, Thou art worthy to take the book, and to open the seals thereof: for thou was slain, and hast redeemed us to God by thy blood out of every kindred, and tongue, and people, and nation; And has made us unto our God kings and priest: and we shall reign on the earth.*

*And I beheld, and I heard the voice of many angels round about the throne and the beast and the elders: and the number of them was ten thousand times ten thousand times ten thousand, and thousands of thousands;*

*Saying with a loud voice, worthy is the Lamb that was slain to receive power, and riches, and wisdom, and honor, and glory, and blessings.*

*And every creature which is in heaven, and on the earth, and under the earth, and such as are in the sea, and all that are in them, heard I saying, Blessing, and honor, and glory, and power, to him that sitteth upon the throne, and unto the Lamb forever.*

*And the four beasts said, Amen. And the twenty four elders fell down and worshipped him that liveth forever and ever.*

This is the wording of scripture in Revelations, chapters four and five. The certainty of what is to come in the soon return of Jesus our Lord and savior.

All that this Christian Journey through a fallen world has been leading up to; is this final event that **will** take place at the return of our Lord and Savior.

I have led you through the journey by telling you my own valley and mountain top events, just as I am sure you have had yours so far. Even though our lives take on many, many struggles, we are able to overcome by the "Blood of the Lamb", that these chapters and verses have finalized in my writing.

I have had times when I didn't think I could go on. I have had times when I didn't want to go on. But because of His great plan for my life, he intervened and changed circumstances that led me down a different path.

When we are heading in a direction that we think is where we want to go, or even think that this is our path to go, but things just keep getting in the way, we call them detours. But when God has his plan then there will be a detour in that path.

I felt like I had many detours in my journey, as maybe you have also felt, but when you know Jesus, and you trust his plan for your life, you can be assured that the detour was very necessary for the God perfect plan.

How would I advise you to avoid some of my pitfalls and mistakes?

I think I would say, "Don't let life lead you." They say that the reason we have our life struggles, most of them anyway, is because we do not think like Jesus.

As long as we want what we want, we have problems. If we want whatever Jesus wants for us then it will end as it should.

I was selfish in many ways. I wanted my career that I spoke about in earlier chapters to be what I wanted it to be. Then as life took a change, and my husband that God had for me entered my life, then that path took a different course. Who knows how it could have ended? The real question is why that course so important? And you learn about plans. But I'm sure I wouldn't have found Jesus as my Savior, or then maybe I would have? Only God knows. He knew from the foundation of the world.

My husband and I, like many married couples, had our ups and downs. But that is normal. Look at scripture and you will see the awful events that led so many astray. We started out, both really agreeing on almost all things. Is that true fifty-three years later? I don't think so. One thing is for sure, God had His great purpose and plan for our life.

I will trust and be assured that I am where I was meant to be in 2018. I am doing what I was supposed to be doing in 2018. Life, no matter how rough it may get, and you saw and read that my life took on many toils and snares.

But because I believe in the sovereignty of God, I know that, "*All things work together for good, to those that are called, (love God) to them that are called according to his purpose* (Romans 8:28).

So as you have read this book and see that no matter what happens in your life, there is a purpose and plan that was ordained for your journey. Take comfort in knowing there is a God the father, Jesus the son, and the Holy Spirit, that is real. There is a Heaven and a Hell.

Determine that you go forward and make each day count for him. *He will see you through all your trials and take you through the fire again, and again. He will never leave you or forsake you* (Hebrews 13:5).

"*How great thou art*," as the old hymn says, and as the other old standard, "*Amazing Grace*".

Our great God is both of these.

That's what we, as created beings by our Lord and Savior have. Over and over, and over. *I will forever give him the glory, the honor and worship due his matchless and holy name. There is no other name given under heaven whereby you must be saved* (Acts 4:12). WE may never meet this side of heaven. So I ask again;

Do you know my Savior? Do you know my friend?

This has been "My Christian journey through a fallen world". It's falling faster than any of us can even know.

Take heart in knowing God has his great plan and purpose for your life also. You can know that plan by staying close to the Lord, following the crumbs that you see him dropping and as you hear his words spoken to your heart through scripture.

Don't live afraid. Because God is near. He is just a prayer away.

### Closing Words of Encouragement

All of our life is meant for T*he King and His Kingdom.*

Take heart my friend. Even though we are living in a fallen world, I hope my true story of my Christian journey will help you know our lives are not in vain. They have a purpose right up to the end.

Living for Jesus, that's my life, until He calls me home.

# ABOUT THE AUTHOR

Sarah lives in the Ozarks, an area of fields and streams, with her husband of 53 years. Her and husband Lanty have 2 grown boys. One 51 and one 37. One awesome grandchild.

She has been a Real Estate Broker for over 25 years but has always enjoyed writing.

Sarah is active in her church, sings in the choir and loves her ministry in the prayer group.

She has always felt the need to bring out the greatest potential of all she becomes involved with, and wants to continue writing and ministering for her Lord and Savior Jesus Christ.

Sarah's website/blog: sarahtylerauthor.com
Facebook: facebook.com/sarah.tyler.7
Other websites: https://sarahtylerrealtyllc.com

SARAH TYLER

CPSIA information can be obtained
at www.ICGtesting.com
Printed in the USA
LVHW081727100419
613663LV00018B/968/P